Our greatest challenge as Christians is to know intimately, the God we call our Father. "This is eternal life."
(John 17:3)

Knowing God Personally 1

THE INTIMATE DIMENSION

Copyright ©2020 Godson Hez
All rights reserved. First paperback edition printed 2020 in the United Kingdom. A catalogue record for this book
is available from the British Library.
ISBN 978-1-913455-17-0
No part of this book shall be reproduced or transmitted in any form or by any means, electronic or mechanical, including photocopying, recording, or by any information retrieval system without prior written permission of the publisher.
Published by Scribblecity Publications.
Printed in Great Britain.
Although every precaution has been taken in the preparation of this book, the publisher and author assume no responsibility for errors or omissions. Neither is any liability assumed for damages resulting from the use of this information contained herein.
Scripture quotations marked NLT are taken from the
Holy Bible, New Living Translation, copyright © 1996, 2004, 2015 by Tyndale House Foundation. Used by permission of Tyndale House Publishers, Inc., Carol Stream, Illinois 60188. All rights reserved.

Dedication

"And this is life eternal, that they might know Thee the only true God, and Jesus Christ, whom Thou hast sent". So, I gladly dedicate this work to all that have taken heed to this end-time call:

- to withdraw from religion into fellowship in God's presence;
- to withdraw from religious activities into kingdom life actualization, and
- to all who sit down daily to learn under the School of the Holy Spirit, seeking for nothing but to know God by revelation.

CONTENTS

Introduction	2
The Source	8
The Divine Order	22
The Dream	36
The Revelation	43
The Knowledge	67
The Confirmation	94
The Mystery	109
The Power	128

INTRODUCTION

The Lord gave me a dream, gave the interpretation, and sent a message to the body of Christ. This dream occurred within the last week of August 2006. For very obvious reasons which I explained hereafter, I could not keep track of the particular day. You will get to understand.

In my first book titled **"FRESH FROM THE ALTAR"** I recorded a dream I had on the 9th of February 2003, where I was caught up into the third heaven and was ushered into the inner court that houses the Ark of the Covenant. The bone-crushing experience it left in me made it impossible for me to forget the day, though I never wrote the date down anywhere except when I started writing the book.

This time, the Lord decided to send another life-transforming dream in a very unusual manner. Though when I went into the scriptures as the Lord explained the meaning of the dream, I discovered that it only appeared to me as unusual, but not to God who moves in diverse ways to perform His wonders. The reason why this divine visitation appeared unusual to me was because of how casual and normal it appeared to be. It was like one having a dream, which was a replay of normal daily life. So, I did not bother myself writing it down immediately until the Lord confronted me days after.

Days after, when I began to write it down in response to God's instruction, I had already lost memory of the particular date I had the dream. Meanwhile, I began to experience the bone-crushing visitation of God as He gave the revelation knowledge accompanying this casual but pregnant dream. The impact has been more tremendous than the first dream I had. Indeed, His ways are past finding out. You too, are about to contact a greater visitation of God as you go through this book.

I must therefore earnestly plead with you not to fall into the same error as I did. If you must avoid being trapped by the same mistake of despising the dream as a normal thing which I am recounting, you have to be patient and humble enough to read through the book. The Lord that sent the dream while He gave His beloved sleep, came back to explain everything to the minutest detail, because of you and me. The book is not about the dream or the dreamer; it is about God and what the Spirit of the Lord is saying to the Body of Christ in this last lap of the end-times. While I was putting the work together, the Lord in His infinite wisdom sent me a confirmation through another source. He settled all my doubts perfectly.

By the way, if you are one of those who do not believe nor regard dreams and revelations generally, I sat where you are sitting now for many years of my Christian faith-walk, until the Heavens had mercy on me. The Lord has brought me into very awesome experiences in recent times exposing the fact that we cannot do without dreams, visions, revelations and trances in these last days. Doing without them is like having computers in this electronic age and yet keeping so many paper files as usual. Sounds crazy, doesn't it?

So many of us have remained where we are because we are not willing to pay the price to tap into heaven's secrets. What price Sir? Consider the following:

- Staying in His presence;
- Living the Altar life;
- Enrolling into the School of the Holy Spirit;
- Keeping a daily covenant time alone with God.

Do they make any sense? Are we familiar with those Christian experiences? Please, if those terms do not sound very familiar, that means, you are not acquainted with such daily Christian habits. Then, you need help; please, get in touch with the author fast. You cannot go a day longer without these experiences. If we do not observe this practical, intimate program of Christian relationship with God, we will end up the same kind of 'nominal Christians' that we see everywhere today. What kind of Christians do we mean? People who are saved from sin but lost into religion. What a great tragedy! The devil has often employed this wicked strategy to take us from one level of slavery into a more subtle one. This book is a wake-up call.

INTRODUCTION

Prophet Joel foretold that in the last days, dreams, visions, revelations and trances will be used frequently by the Spirit of God to speak to God's sons and daughters (Joel 2:28). The early Apostles were helped so much in their ministry through this radical move of God. It was said of Paul the Apostle that he lived his Christian life daily in the abundance of revelations (2 Cor 12:7). No wonder, he excelled greatly. When you see what others cannot see, you do what others cannot do.

Peradventure you don't understand what dreams, visions, revelations, trances and the like means, I recommend Rick Joyner's books - "The Final Quest", "The Call", and many other such revelation books to you. It is not within the scope of this book.

KNOWLEDGE OF GOD

Who on earth stands qualified to tell another about God, except to whom He is revealed? The things you will gain in this book are born out of divine revelation. "… for the Spirit searcheth all things, yea, the deeper things of God. For what man knoweth the things of a man, save the spirit of man which is in him? Even so the things of God knoweth no man, but the Spirit of

God. Now, we have received, not the Spirit of the world, but the Spirit which is of God; that we might know the things that are freely given to us of God, which things we speak (I bring to you through this book), not in the words which man's wisdom teaches, but which the Holy Ghost teaches (1 Cor 2: 10-13). Dare to believe me.

The message is bigger than the messenger. This is why I took time to explain how I came about it or better stated, how the message came about in the first segment of the book. The dream, the interpretation and the message the Lord desires to pass across to the church in the subsequent parts will definitely leave no trace of doubt in you that our God has spoken once again to those who have ears. Thank God, you are one of them. You will discover too that I am only one example of those unprofitable servants in this whole project. I have only done my master's bidding. God bless you.

1
THE SOURCE

TO WHOM GOD IS REVEALED

I do not know whether you have taken time to read through the activities of the devil and his human agents in the end-times as revealed to Daniel in the land of captivity. It presents a very horrifying and devastating sight such that you will be left wondering like Prophet Joel, "…and who can abide (stand) it? (2:11).

In the midst of such consuming fear and seemingly hopeless situations presented in Daniel's revelation is a consolation in Chapter 11:32. This scripture says that while those that do wickedly against the covenant shall be corrupted by flatteries, the people that do know their God shall be strong and do exploits. What privileged, peculiar persons (people) this group of people must be: doing exploits while others are messed up? Who are these peculiar set of people, and what is the secret behind their power? It must be very interesting to belong to this peculiar set of people. So, let us get this revelation knowledge first. It will help us to position our heart for this revelation from God.

As I meditated over the interpretations of this revelation, comparing them with the scriptural verses given to me through the inner impressions of the Holy Spirit, my attention was seriously tickled as the Holy Spirit broke down this second part of that scripture: "…the people that do know their God shall be strong, and do exploits" (Dan. 11:32). Follow me as the Holy Spirit broke it down into three parts for a practical understanding:

a. The people that do know their God: This knowledge here is personified. It is definitely beyond the general knowledge of God as we can deduce from the phrase 'know their God'. It will become clearer when you compare this scripture with our focal text on the cover page which says that, "no one knows the Father, except those to whom the Son wills to reveal Him" (Matt.11:27). The book of Daniel must then be talking about the people (or that person) to whom God has been revealed; the person who receives a personal, revelation knowledge of God. Wow! Only this kind of revelation knowledge of God is capable of taking one beyond the general, conception level of understanding of the person of God, to a personal, perception level of understanding God's will and mind in every situation and at all times. Daniel himself was a practical case study (Dan 2:19-22). So, that part of the scripture simply says, 'those to whom God is revealed...'

b. They shall be strong: Meaning that those people to whom God has been revealed (those in group 'a') are the people in whom the strength of God is revealed. This is the reason they will manifest unusual, undauntable strength that keeps them stable and secured in the face of all turbulences. (Dan 3:16-18). So, 'those to whom God is revealed are those in whom the strength of God is revealed...'

c. And do exploits: Meaning that those through whom the power of God will be manifested in the form of exploits are only those that know their God. They are the people to whom God has been revealed; they shall be strong as the revelation knowledge of God reveals the strength of God in them. They are the only people through whom the power of God is revealed. (Dan 3:24-29). What a mystery!

Summarily therefore, that Bible verse as revealed by Daniel could be illuminated further to read: the people to whom God is revealed are the people in whom God is revealed, and becomes the people through whom God is revealed. The truth then is that God can never be revealed through us until He has been revealed to us and in us. This is the mystery of Godliness.

Brother Paul presents a perfect picture of a man to whom, in whom and through whom God is revealed. He never had the privilege of following the Lord Jesus through the length and breadth of Galilee and Jerusalem, yet, his strength and exploits in the kingdom business remains outstanding. How did he come about this? It all started when the Lord revealed Himself to him in Acts 9:1-8; then in Gal 1:16, he testified of the Father revealing Jesus in him (Paul), propelling him with grace to preach Him (Jesus) among the heathen, not conferring with flesh and blood. He never saw or had any need after this revelation, to return to Jerusalem, to them which were Apostles before him, but went straight into Arabia, to Damascus, then Jerusalem and on and on as the Spirit led him (Gal1:17-18). This was responsible for the undeniable proofs of God's revelation through him all over the New Testament. To Him, in Him, and through him, God was and is still revealed. We will see more of his testimonies in subsequent chapters. The whole essence of this book is that we may know Him by revelation beyond what we are being told or taught about Him.

What a perfect picture of a complete Christian presented in this scriptural verse (Dan 11:32). At the bedrock of every Christian experience is this undaunting, propelling, personal revealed knowledge of God that no man can gainsay. Only a truly born-again Christian can bear witness to this. Think about this. Oh! The confidence it breeds is unchallenging (Heb 3:14). My prayer is that after going through this book God will find in us worthy vessels to whom, in whom and through whom He will be revealed. This is the whole essence of our Christian faith; coming to that point where we can begin to enjoy a dynamic, exciting relationship with God.

LEARN OF ME

Globally, every ardent learner from real life experiences will agree with me that the greatest asset of a man in this world is the wealth of his knowledge. Every other asset, financial or material acquired by a man can grow wings anytime and fly away, but not his wealth of knowledge. The man's knowledge lives on with him and dies with him. A man may possess the best of gifts or talents, but they will remain latent and unprofitable until the presence of such gifts is acknowledged and put to effective use. We therefore quickly discover that in all life's pursuits, secular or spiritual, every man is:

a. Limited in life by the level of knowledge in his mind

b. Shaped by the worth (value) of his knowledge, and

c. Made by the quality and quantity of his applied knowledge.

In the light of this understanding, if our knowledge of God is shallow, our lives will never be able to reflect true Christianity and we are never going to be able to impact our world for Christ.

In our spiritual life, it poses a great danger to be negatively affected by these three success determinants in life's pursuits. This is why God lamented against His children in Hosea 4:1 "For the Lord has controversy against the inhabitants of the land, because there is no truth…nor knowledge of God in the land." Paul also lamented about the people of God having great zeal, but not according to knowledge (Rom.10:1, 2). Our Lord Jesus Christ puts it more succinctly that, "This is eternal life, that they might know You, the true God" (Jn 17: 3), and in Matt 22:29, He rebuked the people saying "Ye do err, not knowing the scriptures, nor the power of God."

Brethren, it is so alarming and heart-breaking to still hear God lament again about the lack of His knowledge in this dispensation of "seemingly vast increases in knowledge." The disposition we all wear, just like the Old Testament Rabbis, suggests we are so saturated with the knowledge of the Lord. In fact, we have no need that any should teach us. We all dine and wine with the Master. The Holy Spirit, who is come to teach us all things sees no teachable heart (1 Jn 2:27).

Yet, this our superficial disposition is greatly challenged and opposed by the absence of:

- The inner, unshakable courage and strength that stems from the personal knowledge of the Father.
- This transparent, sober, gracious and Godly lifestyle that attests to His revelation knowledge alone and no other source.
- The genuine heaven-inspired exploits that draw down revival and inspires Godly reverence among men around us.
- The fear of God that is characterized by a humble submission to one another in Christian love as we saw in the early church.

Think about it? Is there any trace of the fear of God in men of our generation? How can anybody fear God when those of us who claim knowledge of Him misrepresent Him by our speeches and actions, as a carefree God who does not mind whether we fear Him or not.

I am involved, brethren. If not for the weight of His revelation that gave the inspiration to this book, I am the least of mortals to bring you this message. The true knowledge of the Father will make nonsense of our claims and place us where we rightly belong. We are still unprofitable earthen vessels, whose only value is the one placed on us by the manifold grace of the Father. The message that God is bringing to us through this book is just one of the exciting privileges of God's end-time visitation. Oh, what a grace to have God share secrets with the least of mortals.

If we must be profited by this timely message, don't hurry through it, please. We must see ourselves through the pages of the book. We must come down from whatever pinnacle we have placed ourselves on and put on the Jesus disposition: "Learn of Me, for I am meek and lowly in heart..." (Matt 11:29). Learning is one undisputable source of real knowledge; yet our modern-day Christianity is fraught with great opposition to learning. Don't forget brethren, there is no graduation on this side of heaven as far as spiritual matters are concerned. "For we know in part, and prophesy in part" (1 Cor. 13:9). Incidentally, the part we do not know often lies with the unsuspecting, unexpected, unqualified ants (Prvb 6:8) and asses (Num 22:27-31). This explains the reason why God keeps coming from unexpected sources most times to do unexpected things. What a God with whom we have to do! Some relevant timely messages also lie in the mouth of the ass. What a source, you may wonder? Ask Balaam!

WATCH OUT FOR THE ASSES

When the experienced High Priest of Shiloh became dim both in sight and revelation knowledge, God had no choice but to turn to the young, inexperienced Samuel (1 Sam 3: 4-21). When the experienced and famous prophet Balaam could no longer see and discern the voice of God, God was left with no choice, but to open the vocal chords of the ass and gave it a voice to speak (Num 22:23 – 30). How sober the prophet must have become after the ass spoke sense into him, and the Lord opened his eyes to see what the poor ass has seen a long time before him. Do you blame Balaam? Who is the 'ass' after all to be used of God to reveal divine secrets? Sure, we stand on good ground now to appreciate Balaam's 'wisdom.'

Many years after Balaam, a similar thing happened. Peter (The Rock) and the rest of the Apostles were in their hide-outs after the crucifixion of Jesus Christ, and Mary Magdalene whom both the Apostles and the religious Pharisees had written off as unqualified for heaven brought the resurrection message to the apostles. You know the rest of the story, but you must hear this first: "Now when Jesus was risen early.... He appeared first to Mary Magdalene, out of whom He had cast seven devils. And she went and told them (the disciples), that had been with Him, as they mourned and wept. And when they had heard that he was alive and had been seen of her, believed not" (Mark 16:9-11). What can we learn from this act of the disciples?

Though they had been with Him, they all went mourning hopelessly after the death of Jesus. Even when the news of the resurrection came, the source was very doubtful; another ass speaking, another expensive news from the manger, another revival news from the unqualified Mary Magdalene. "What a source!" They wondered. Watch out brethren, the ass made sense after all; the Mary resurrection message was real after all. What a God whom we deal with; whose ways are far beyond our comprehension! The Apostles were left with no choice later but to join the Mary league. This book in your hands has brought great revival into the lives of so many Christians, young and old since its first publication. You are about to come in contact with that same grace.

DOES THIS AFFECT US?

Brethren we should be convinced by now that we are all sitting where these ones sat. It is wisdom to learn from the mistakes of others. God is at it again. The Father is still in the business of using the foolish things of the world so that no flesh can glory before HIM. He is the revealer of secrets, and He uses whom He chooses. It will take a man partnering with the Holy Spirit not to despise the voices of the asses and the Marys of our time.

So many people might be tempted to miss the revelations in this book simply because the author is not a very familiar or popular name; not one of the Bishops, not a T.V. star-preacher and not even a G.O. of one of the loudest congregations, nor one of the notable 'miracle workers'. Most often, when we organize programmes that require outside preachers we look for the high and popular, at the expense of the spiritual impact desired to be made.

This is one great plague that has hindered man's ability to access divine secrets. We have often been pre-emptive of the move of God. We keep missing His revelation or visitations, because we expect Him as the mighty rushing wind; we keep expecting the cry of the newborn king from the Palace and not the manger. The message is often lost in our fruitless bid to reconcile the wretched background of the messenger with the expensive message he is carrying. Consider this:

WHO ARE YOU?

When John the Baptist came to announce and to prepare the people for the coming of the Lord Jesus Christ, he ministered with so much unction and anointing. He ministered fearlessly under the powerful influence of the Holy Spirit, being overwhelmed by the revelation knowledge of the message he carried. Though his message was different from the normal, making him as it were a lonely voice, the power of his personal knowledge of the mission propelled him. The result was overwhelming. Many "went to him from Jerusalem, and all Judea, and the entire region round about Jordan…confessing their sins" (Matt 3: 5, 6). What a revival!

Yet in the midst of this revival, what bothered some religious leaders was the personality and background of John: The Jews sent Priests and Levites from Jerusalem to ask Him, "Who are you? …what sayest thou of thyself?" He answered them, "I am the voice of one crying in the wilderness …make straight the way of the Lord…" (Jn 1: 19-22, 23). He returned them to the message that mattered most. "What do you mean, John?" They must have asked in bewilderment. Oh brethren, I mean that the message is not about me the messenger it is all about the 'message' I am come to deliver. Dare to believe me. The secret that gave John this strong voice, against every intimidating attempt is what God is about exposing here. Dare to be humble enough to get this secret; it is not about the messenger.

2
THE DIVINE ORDER

Men and Brethren, as the Lord took me through some experiences towards achieving this course; I have come to discover that everything about heaven follows a divine order, unmistakably controlled by the invisible but very real hands of God. Every movement along the right course produces a corresponding result. Nobody sleeps and wakes up suddenly accessing great Christian experiences without going through the corresponding right precepts.

NOTE:
What do I mean by great Christian experiences? I don't mean the very questionable, entertaining Christian displays paraded here and there in the name of Christian gifting(s). You don't need to keep any

order to get there. You don't even need any sense of discipline. You can always know them by their firm hold unto evil habits, while professing and displaying their Christian experiences (Matt 7:16,21-23).

So, it was awesome as the Father took me through the necessary divine order to access this divine knowledge. In His infinite wisdom, He decided as always, to make me a first partaker of the secret He purposed to use me to share. I did not plan the order. I only followed Him each step of the way, only to realize later that He was the One that ordered my steps.

Recall that I said in the introduction that I owe you a brief explanation of how this dream came about. The aim is to save you the problem of falling into the same error I was a victim of. My error was that I never took the dream serious because it looked so casual and normal. Thank God, He came to me again, this time while I was awake. My saving grace was my embrace of divine order for accessing heaven's secrets; that is, having time alone with God.

ALONE WITH GOD

One day in the year 2003, I resorted to a lonely suburb

of Lagos where I stayed most times to receive divine dictations that gave birth to the book **"FRESH FROM THE ALTAR"**(Revised Edition: Fresh Fire for Fresh Result). That day was exceptional as the Lord dealt with me in a very unusual manner.

God began to help me that day to understand that if only we can discover for ourselves His mind, His will, His thoughts and His plan for us as individuals early in life, it will save us from many struggles and wasted years. What made the day very unusual was my deep and serious contention with the Holy Spirit. While I pleaded my cause to the heavens resisting and refuting every call to write inspirational books, the Father was busy giving me book titles to work on. I won't bother us with details of my dialogue with the Father on that day, but this book title was one of the topics He outlined. He conquered me for good, after all that.

Though I listed the topic among others, yet I never took God seriously, because I felt I didn't 't stand qualified to write on a topic such as this. Questions trooped in and out of my heart: who am I in the book of 'who is who' among Christian teachers and theologians? How many years have I been in Christian service? How much of God do I know to earn me the ability to teach others about knowing God personally? I don't intend to bore you, dear reader with stories of God's personal dealings with me, but I need you to understand and tap into this grace. This work is beyond mental exercise. Even if I am to sleep and wake up with a topic to write on, it will certainly be very different from this. Only divine guidance got me into enrolling in the School of God's presence. This singular move made this work possible.

What do I mean? While I was in God's presence on that fateful day as He interpreted the dream, He made a nonsense of everything I wrote down from my research in preparation for this book. He made me cancel and trash the scripts I had been putting together for years, because they never made sense beyond what we are used to – the general, peripheral knowledge of the Father which has made us remain perpetual aliens in our Father's land.

The Lord led me through deeper knowledge of Him in His omniscient presence which prepared the way for this divine encounter in August 2006. I had never experienced God at this deeper dimension in my twenty six years as a born-again Christian. He knew that if only I had the literal and technical qualifications, plus the long pastoral service and experience needed to do the normal, I would have ran ahead of Him to produce the book; though it was not going to make an impact beyond the normal, mental knowledge that we are used to. So, this divine arrangement first ushered me into great experiences in His presence. I urge you therefore dear reader, to patiently hear a little about this divine move that brought me into another level of true kingdom life in God's presence. Heaven came down and filled my life with God's glory.

The first dealings of God with me when I started this school in His presence was to convict and convince me that our claims as children of God remain very doubtful considering how sparingly we appear in the presence of the God we call our Father. We deny Him the pleasure of a consistent, sweet Father and son/daughter communion, and deny ourselves the impartation of His revelation knowledge. It was never meant to be this way from the beginning. Adam and Eve – our first parents had great times in His presence in the cool of the evening (Gen. 3:8). You remember we are all created for His pleasure (Rev. 4:11), but how often do we deny Him this pleasure?

I thought I was doing very well with the few minutes I gave in my quiet times until it was introduced to me as a school in God's presence. The consciousness of the fact that I am seated under the best teacher and the willingness to learn daily under His tutelage made the great difference. The disciplinary life of punctuality, attentiveness and dedication on my part as a good student, and the way and manner the Spirit-Teacher began to paint the words of the Bible to me as a baby at those solitary times in His presence made the experiences heaven on earth. My God! I suddenly began to look forward to that time each day, just like a child falling in love with her class teacher would always pray that every day becomes a school day. Wow! The difference it made in my life and ministry was as clear and transforming as Isaiah's experience in Isaiah 6:1-8.

WHAT ABOUT THIS SCHOOL

Remember that the Holy Spirit was introduced to the church as our Teacher and Comforter. This school is an opportunity willingly created by a believer to learn as a student under the Spirit of the Living God. It is a discipleship programme undertaken by God through the undisputable teaching ministry of the Holy Spirit in this end-time. Our addiction to religion has denied us the awesome, very relevant ministry of the Holy Spirit today! What is this school about to achieve?

a. It is the means through which the Father will move to both search and seek out the Lord's flock (Ezek 34: 11-12). Only when the sheep get acquainted with the shepherd's voice can they hear and follow Him.
b. The school is out to make Christian believers into disciples indeed (Jn 8:32), by continuing in the Word.
c. The training is meant to get believers fully conformed into the image of Christ (Rom 8:29).
d. The school is meant for the cleansing, perfecting and adornment of the Bride of Christ (Eph. 5:25-27; Rev. 19:7, 8) through undiluted word revelations. Are you a member of the Bride of Christ?
e. The school is out to restore and revive today's dead church back to life again (Ezek 37:1-14), to establish her on the top of the mountains and exalt her above the hills to become the envy of this heathen generation

(Isa 2:2).

Brethren, this is a mountain top experience. You can't beat this move; it is very simple, yet very real and result oriented. Truly, the Lord's yoke is easy and His burden, so light (Matt 11:30). Our greatest burden today is the one laid on us by religion; being promoted by the vendors of 'another gospel' (Gal. 1:6, 7) – the Rabbis of this generation, who will soon face the Father's judgment. Just a quick return to the gospel of grace which is made real and personal by the revelation of Christ will convince you.

Paul testified in Gal 1:11, 12 that the gospel which he preached is not after man, neither did he receive it nor was taught it by man, but by the revelation of Jesus Christ. To the Ephesian Church, he further testified in Eph 3:3, 4 how that by revelation, God made known unto him the mystery (… so that when you read, you may understand my knowledge in the mystery of Christ). The question we should be asking ourselves is this: 'is this knowledge of mysteries in Christ an exclusive privilege of Paul's and the early church?

The answer of course is 'Not at all'. The following verses 5 and 6 added that this knowledge of the mysteries (secrets of God), though "not made known unto the sons of men in other ages past, is now revealed unto his holy Apostles and prophets by the Spirit. That the Gentiles (you and me) should be fellow heirs, and of the same body, and partakers of His promise in Christ by the gospel."

This is a divine order, put in place by the Spirit to accommodate whosoever wills (John 3:16) into the new covenant. Brethren, all our inheritance in the Lord Jesus Christ does not begin and end in material riches and physical protection. The greater part of our privileged inheritance in Christ is this access into the knowledge of mysteries (divine secrets) of God through the revelation of His Spirit. I keyed into this grace, and I make bold to testify that nothing else could have granted me this access into the divine secrets revealed in this book. You too are about to give your own testimony as you tap into this divine order.

ORDERED STEPS

May the Lord order your steps! Though we may not

understand it sometimes, and might find it painful taking some steps as ordered by God, but at the end of every experience, we will discover that every step He took us through was worth the while. This is the heritage of every Christian pilgrim. This is the reason I am getting you acquainted with how God ordered my steps into this revelation!

At the time God connected me to this end-time discipleship programme, I was already completely dissatisfied with the religion which today's church is fast settling for, and I had a burning hunger for revival. Unconsciously brethren, this provided a divine platform that resulted in this encounter. Now I know that no matter the negative pressure against our true faith, every hunger for God's righteousness must be filled (Matt 5:6).

It's a choice we all must make. The Father is willing to make known unto us the mystery (secret) of His will (concerning every aspect of our lives), according to His good pleasure which He hath purposed in Himself (Eph.1:9). However, if you are satisfied with how and where you are, you may not get the best out of His presence. This is beyond our normal observation of quiet time or morning devotions, though, they could be complementary. The difference is that in this Holy Spirit-led, Discipleship School some order must be observed. For example:

1. You must be diligent to keep it at a particular time of the day, hence it is a school. This time is called 'Covenant Time.' Feel free to change the time when necessitated by the changing schedules of your daily activities, and in agreement with your Teacher – The Holy Spirit.
2. You must be very consistent and very punctual.
3. Remember that the school is located wherever you can guarantee uninterrupted quietness within that appointed time.
4. Remember also that the Holy Spirit is the Teacher while you are the disciple (student). It is not a time for prayers except if the Holy Spirit prompts you intermittently as you are studying.
5. Enter His presence with great delight and desire to hear God speak to you, and not with an attitude of one being unduly compelled.
6. Your study materials are your Bible and books

written out of revelation knowledge and not just religious and theological knowledge. Some books are recommended on the last page of this book.

Note: We are very good at being the ones always talking to God at all times. Each time we come to God, we are always the ones talking to Him. We hardly hear Him speaking, because we are never prepared in the first place to listen to Him. Yet He has so much to tell us and He itches to communicate with us on a daily basis. Give Him this time and don't turn it to another prayer meeting. Be still in His presence and learn as He speaks. This was the secret that released grace and positioned me for the impartation of this secret. Our much desired end-time revival cannot come until we are endued with the revelation knowledge of the Father. This is not a product of theological knowledge.

When you get the books as recommended, you will understand better. Feel free to get in touch if you need help. All I did was to embrace this move, and the Heavens opened up, and till today, great revelations, dreams and visions have not ceased from pouring down. Bad habits were broken off, grace is being released on daily basis; I have rest in His presence. What a glorious estate! Come on with me greatly beloved.

CALL TO REST

There is a rest that is remaining unto the saints (Heb 4:9). In other words, a part of the rest has been given to us. This is the rest given to us at salvation Matt 11:28: The remaining part of the rest is found, not given. You will find the remaining part of this rest as you begin to sit down consistently, learning at Jesus' feet. As we stay in His presence daily, heaven's secrets are released unto us, we get relieved of the religious, traditional and environmental burdens, we exchange them with the light burdens of Christ and become yokefellows with Jesus, then we find rest for our souls (Matt 11:29). At this point, it is difficult to look back by reason of the yoke binding you with Jesus. At this point, your hand is sufficiently and gladly on the plow and sees no cause to look back (Luke 9:62).

Anything you seek and find, you guard jealously, anything that is given to you can easily be lost, because you may not know its value. This is the point where most Christians come to and stop. They only receive the first part of the rest given to them at salvation. If you stop at salvation, laying the foundation of repentance on a daily basis you can backslide anytime. But the second part of the rest which you find for your soul, you can hardly trade off for anything, because you know what it took you to get there and will value it greatly. Hence Paul admonished us to leave the peripheral level of His rest and enter the next and more secure level: "Let us labour therefore to enter into His rest" (Heb4:11). May you find rest for your soul today!

3

THE DREAM

A PLEASANT MYSTERY

I had this dream during the early hours within the last week of August 2006. I did not keep track of the particular day, because I did not record this dream when it came. One striking thing that happens immediately you begin to observe your covenant time consistently and diligently with the Holy Spirit is the flood of divine revelations that will begin to come to you through dreams and visions. The interpretations were also given with the help of the Holy Spirit. Remember that this all depends on the level of our sincere commitment to learning and exercising ourselves in line with the instructions of our Teacher in this school. This is the same thing that happens under our secular education.

When you begin to spend time consistently in God's

presence, please take your dreams serious. They are not ordinary. You should be able to learn from my own mistake. Though I recorded other dreams and interpretations at those periods as illuminated by the Holy Spirit, when this one came, my inclination was not to write it down. May God deliver us from our own rigid mindsets in this Kingdom business. "For my thoughts are not your thoughts, neither are your ways my ways, saith the Lord. For as the heavens are higher than the earth, so are my ways higher than your ways and my thoughts than your thoughts" (Isa 55:8,9). This is very, very serious, especially, considering the fact that we are expected to live our daily lives in total conformity with His ways and thoughts. Think about it.

In other words, this wide gap that exists between our thought patterns and that of God must be bridged if we must access His thoughts and be acquainted with His ways. It indeed presents a pleasant mystery. Neither our learning from a distance, nor a peripheral, general knowledge of God will bridge this gap. It is only as we dwell in His presence, beholding as in a glass the glory of the Lord, that we are changed into the same image from glory to glory (bridging the wide gap), even as by the Spirit of the Lord (2 Cor. 3:18). This is what makes the mystery a pleasant one.

So, as I kept consistently having a good time in His presence, the Lord confronted me few days later. As I sat up that morning to learn at His feet, He brought the memory of this dream back, and asked me to begin to write it down, because it was not as casual and normal as I thought. Thank God, He knew where to find me, in the cool of the morning. I would have missed the divine opportunity that gave birth to this revelation. Thank God for the Covenant Time.

A NATION IN TOTAL DARKNESS

In this dream, the whole nation was thrown into darkness. This darkness lasted for so long, not just hours, but for many days. The general source of power in that dream called National Electric Power Authority (NEPA), in Nigeria was completely paralyzed. It was a national problem, but the picture of the nation presented in that dream spans beyond the geographical bounds of Nigeria. It was as if the darkness went beyond Nigeria and NEPA was the controlling source of all the power.

The picture in that dream was a very horrible, disappointing and depressing one. NEPA had tried their best, but the best they could achieve was a very epileptic supply; a situation worse than the power supply we have currently in Nigeria, as at the time of writing this book. My prayer is that the power supply situation will change for good in the nearest future in Jesus name, Amen!

Business activities and life generally became so unpleasant and worrisome in that dream. Those that could afford it went to buy their personal generating sets. So, they had relief. They were happy and more relaxed than the rest of the population that depended on the general source of electricity called NEPA. In that dream, I happened to be one of those that had a generating set; so, myself and my family were happy. However, the majority could not afford a generating set. So, there was serious confusion in the land. It was in this state of confusion and perplexity that besieged the nation that I woke up.

Now, does this not present a perfect picture of the electricity supply situation in Nigeria (at least from my childhood till year 2007 when this book was written). If you were in my shoes residing in Nigeria at a time like this, would you have given a second thought to this kind of dream as having any spiritual connotation? Again, just as I was one of the few that owned a generating set in the dream, I also own a Gen-set in the real world. Can you now appreciate the predicament I found myself in? I was tempted to think this dream mirrored the apparent situation around us. We all know that sometimes our dreams come as reflections or replays of our activities during the day. But this case was different.

The Father only decided to use the known to reveal the unknown mysteries of the kingdom. So that 'he that readeth may understand'. So, this was where I sat for many days before He visited again; this time while I was awake. Before I go into the interpretation, I want to summarize the dream, highlighting the salient points, for our clearer understanding of the dream's interpretation.

NOTE THE FOLLOWING POINTS:

1. Everybody helplessly depended on NEPA for the supply of power for illumination.

2. NEPA means National Electric Power Authority (now Power Holding Corporation – PHCN).

3. NEPA had done her best to ensure a good and consistent supply of light, but her best was only as good as the epileptic supply in Nigeria today (that is, as at the time of this revelation because I am believing God for a change in our power supply situation).

4. The dream presented Nigeria as a global village. In other words, this unsatisfactory light situation extended beyond the geographical Nigeria. This was further buttressed by the use of National Electric Power Authority instead of the current Power Holding Corporation of Nigeria. The latter name specified Nigeria while the former speaks of National which makes it relevant for understanding the message that the Father is bringing to us.

5. The situation presented a paralyzing circumstance on the economy, and brought about real anguish, worry and a state of hopelessness among the populace.

6. Only the very few that could afford personal generating sets were happy, relieved, and relaxed, and

were also confident to keep life afloat.

7. Those that had generating sets felt so relaxed and relieved despite the cost of running the generating sets.

I think we are now in a position to understand and appreciate the wisdom of God in the interpretation of this dream. Our God is simply too much. "What a dream!" I am sure we are rightly positioned having come this far to appreciate and understand the wisdom of God in this revelation.

4

THE REVELATION

"At that time Jesus answered and said, "I thank Thee, Oh Father, Lord of Heaven and Earth, because thou hast hid these things from the wise and prudent, and hast revealed them unto babes. Even so, Father; for so it seemed good in Thy sight... No man knoweth the Son but the Father, neither knoweth any man the Father, save the Son, and **he to whomsoever the Son will reveal him.**

(Matt 11:25-27).

It is important to note at this point before we get into the interpretation of this dream that when God confides information to us in coded forms, such as parables, dreams, trances or signs, the intention is not to keep us in the dark regarding the issue. It is the joy of every teacher in the secular world seeing a student coming back for explanations of what the student did not understand. So, we should feel free to go to God to ask Him for explanations to our dreams and all His communication that appears coded to us. We have this rare privilege in this dispensation. This book is precisely a product of one of such rare privileges of making the Father's mind known to the church by revelation. Keep this scriptural text at the beginning of the chapter in your memory as we go through the revelation.

Brethren, it was such a startling experience as I sat a few days after the dream to observe my covenant time, and God began to interpret the dream line upon line. After writing it down as I was instructed by the 'Teacher' (sure you understand Him now), He began to explain everything to the minutest detail. Every word and sentence made meaning, and nothing was left to doubt or confusion. What wisdom! 'What a revelation!

I must quickly remind us at this point that these interpretations were neither premeditated, nor given by me. They were stated here as I received them from divine impressions. It was similar to the disciples standing before Jesus as He explained to them the parable of the sower in (Matt 13:18-23). I was awake and seated in His presence as He spoke. I also wrote down in my diary while the Lord ministered. Some of the scriptural verses attached to the interpretations were given to me directly as the Lord spoke, while some others were gotten by me as I personally searched the scriptures to confirm the various interpretations given. So, let us start from the major and paramount object in this dream.

DIVINE INTERPRETATIONS -

THE LIGHT:

This referred to the general light which the whole world depended upon and looked forward to illumination. 'This light', the Lord said, 'represents the Word of God'. This could be seen clearly from the book of Psalm 119:105 saying, "Thy word is a lamp unto my feet, and a light unto my path". In verse 130 of same chapter, the scripture also stated that "the entrance of your (God's) Word giveth light…". In Prov 6:23, (NKJV), it says, "For the commandment is a lamp, and the law a light". Further, in the book of John 1:1-9, we have a New Testament confirmation of what light stands for spiritually. "In the beginning was the Word, and the Word was with God, and the Word was God… In Him was life, and the life was the light of men. And the light shineth in darkness; and the darkness comprehended it not… That was the true light, which lighteth every man that cometh into the world".

You will agree with me that these words of the scripture were so clearly stated and perfectly explained the interpretations. Brethren, the Word of God goes beyond mere letters. The information contained in God's word is illuminating; it is beyond mere stories; it is revealing, it reveals God Himself and the mysteries around His personality.

The entire life of every man born into this world remains as formless, void, and full of darkness (Gen. 1:2), just as the earth was at the beginning. God the Father then spoke, light (illumination), form (shape) and life into it. It was only then that the earth and the seas began to be fruitful. In other words, until God speaks light, shape and life into us, our lives remain void, full of darkness (ignorance), and lifeless (inactive). This fact underscores the choice of words by our Lord Jesus Christ in John 3:3 - 5 to the great teacher and ruler of the Jews (and to every man of whatever status, but without the revelation knowledge of the Father); He says, "Verily verily (Most certainly), I say unto you, except a man be born again, he cannot see (enter) the kingdom of God.

The choice of these words 'being born again' becomes so perfect when considered from this background, that every life at birth is void, without form, and full of darkness. It therefore remains lifeless and a non-entity until the illuminating power of God's word shines into it, dispels the darkness and reveals the Almighty Father. Real life then begins at this point; hence it is referred to as new birth experience. Let me stop this explanation thus far before I begin to write another book on 'The New Birth'.

I am simply overwhelmed by God's revelation knowledge. I am short of words to express this divine impartation. Suffice it to say here my brethren that the more of God's revelation knowledge we have, the more our lives become enlightened, the better and more definite our perception becomes of the issues of life and Godliness. What a glorious estate to achieve.

Having explained to me what light stood for, the Lord drew my attention to the fact that we have two major sources of light in this world. One is the natural light that has its source from the sun, moon and stars; the other source of light is the electrical energy which is one of the man-made, technological developments that has undeniably proved its relevance to man. So, whether natural or the man-made, the importance of light to the human life is enormous. Light enlightens life.

However, for the sake of the message the Lord seeks to pass across to the entire body of Christ, the light in question here is the 'NEPA-LIGHT'. You will highly appreciate God's wisdom in this dream as He systematically exposes the secrets point by point. So, what does NEPA stand for in this dream?

NEPA:

As noted earlier, the acronym NEPA means National Electric Power Authority. Literally, it is the Authority that controls the supply of electricity in Nigeria. Therefore, everybody depends on NEPA for the supply of light. The Lord gave the interpretation thus:

NEPA as seen in this dream represents all the human or man-made instruments that constitute the sources or channels of the knowledge of God's word. Every human channel of divine precepts available to every man born under the heavens constitutes NEPA in this dream.

Now, consider with me those human agents known to us, who constitute the common or general sources of the impartation of the knowledge of God's word. Some of them include:

- Our Parents
- Our Pastors, Bishops, Prophets and preachers with various titles
- Our Christian religious knowledge (CRK) teachers and theological seminary lecturers;
- Our fellow nominal Christians and church workers;
- Our spiritual Christian leaders and mentors;
- Christian recorded messages etc.

These sources and the likes are the NEPA which I saw in the dream as interpreted by the Lord. The implications of these interpretations will be revealed in the latter chapters. They are indeed touching and very profound. We must, however, note at this point some important truths emanating from the interpretation of this dream so far for clearer understanding:

- Just as NEPA supplies physical light, these human instruments too supply spiritual light; that is the knowledge of God's Word.
- Just as the entire citizens looked to NEPA and depended so much on it because of the importance and relevance of their services, so also our Christian world is seriously dependent on the services of those common sources of the knowledge of God, if they must know Him, the only true God.
- Just as the importance of electricity supply and energy cannot be over-emphasized in any society, the importance of a good supply or flow of God's word is much more to be desired.
- Just as the social, economic and technological developments of any nation or society are anchored on the stability of power supply, every exploit expected of Christians of all ages is anchored on a consistent flow of the undiluted Word of life (the light, the power unto salvation - Rom 1:16).

The irony of it all however is that the dream presented a situation where the body, the source, the controller or the fountain of power – NEPA had done her best, but her best had only remained as epileptic and frustrating as our power supply today in Nigeria. So many individuals and companies had closed down, losing so many assets and investments by reason of the poor power supply in Nigeria as at the time of this revelation. My prayer is that God will help us out of these doldrums (that is, the Nigerian power supply situation). However, God is only using it to pass a more important message across to the Body of Christ that constitutes, nations of heavenly citizens presently scattered all over the world. The church today is suffering the worst mess more as a result of the unwholesome supply of God's Word, than from the physical problems occasioned by the epileptic power supply of any nation.

Having understood what light and NEPA represented, what then is NEPA-Light? Before the Lord explained what NEPA-light stood for, a question bothered me in my heart. But why did the Lord use NEPA? Does this imply that this revelation pertains unto Nigeria alone? Is the revelation only relevant to Christians in Nigeria? I thought about all this within me. As if the Lord heard what was going on in my mind, He took over from my thoughts and began to answer me. "The revelation is not pertaining to Nigeria alone", He said. He went

THE REVELATION

further to explain that "if the situation presented in this dream was about Nigeria alone, I should have used Power Holding Corporation of Nigeria – PHCN. Why? Because the nation 'Nigeria' is specifically stated". Rather, He chose to adopt 'National Electric Power Authority (NEPA)' which suits any nation or people. This made great sense.

It has to be made clear at this point that as at the time of this revelation, the body handling electricity supply in Nigeria was no longer named National Electric Power Authority (NEPA), but had changed their name to Power Holding Corporation of Nigeria (PHCN). Of course, we cannot be more current than God. So, why use the National Electric Power Authority (NEPA)? The Lord said, He decided to use the more liberal acronym – NEPA, because any nation can adopt it. That means, it qualifies well for any nation's electricity supply body. So, the word, 'National' in the acronym 'NEPA' as seen in this dream refers to all nations of the world, not just Nigeria.

Well, we can easily see and appreciate God's wisdom here. Every truth is parallel. What is a Nation? A nation is a people or race organized as a state. In that order, as far as God is concerned, the world is a state. The World as a globe is God's nation. God is the founder, the Architect, the Creator, the Maker, the President, and the Autocrat (Psalm 24:1, 2). This is wisdom. On the other hand, the Christians are God's nation. He is the President and Commander in Chief of the Christian nation. God is the undisputable Chief Executive Officer of the universal body of Christ.

Having understood this, we are now better positioned to appreciate what the word NEPA–Light stood for in that dream.

NEPA LIGHT

NEPA light as given to me by the father's interpretation represents every knowledge of God's word that we have learnt are being taught or that is handed down to us from all the general or common sources of Christian knowledge. Some of those sources have been enumerated under NEPA. The Lord referred all such illumination, or knowledge of God's word acquired from 'NEPA-sources' as 'General knowledge of God'.

In other words, every belief or opinion that we hold about God, about Christianity, Heaven and hell, about Holiness and righteousness, about eternity and man's relationship with God, about sin and corruption, about judgment and the second coming of Christ, and every knowledge emanating and acquired from any other source outside a personal revelation knowledge of the subject matter, such knowledge, opinion or belief so acquired, the Holy Spirit says, are equal to NEPA LIGHT.

Great, wonderful, and in-depth as such knowledge may appear or be, the Lord said it only has a pass mark for 'general knowledge' of Him. Such knowledge is only as good as our NEPA LIGHT, very epileptic, inconsistent, and very unreliable. On such a level of God's knowledge, our personal spiritual perception remains fallow until enhanced with the aid of the Holy Spirit during our personal meditation time in God's presence. General religious knowledge, the Lord says is only peripheral and can only qualify for a preamble to a whole life experience. You cannot plan nor thrive on such a level of knowledge. In case you fall within this NEPA-source category like me; don't throw away the book yet. He that cometh from above, is above all (Jn 3:31). It is time to learn.

As I pondered on this revelation, the Lord understood my confusion and explained further. He gave me an illustration using the three major levels of acquiring secular education; that is, primary, post primary and the University levels. Having been opportuned to pass through these levels, it made so much meaning to me. I received another level of illumination. Here, you discover again that every truth is parallel, and the Father is the source of all truths. Awesome God! As we get into this wonderful illustration, I was caught up in wonder. Think through this with me.

GOD LAMENTS AGAIN

So many thoughts began to flood through my mind at this point as these interpretations progressed. Brethren, I lack words to convey the kind of heaviness that came upon my heart. It could be the kind of divine insight that prompted Paul's heaviness and continual sorrow for his kinsmen in Rom 9:2-3. In his words, "I have great heaviness and continual sorrow in my heart. For I could wish that myself were accursed from Christ for my brethren, my kinsmen according to the flesh". In the next Chapter (10:1), he poured the heaviness out in prayer 'that Israel might be saved!' From what were they to be saved? From sin, poverty, Satan, Babylonian captivity, etc? No way!

Go back to Rom 9:4-5 (Amp. Version) and understand what they are to be saved from. Who were the Israelites? "For they are Israelites, and to them belong God's adoption (as a Nation) and the glorious presence (Shekinah). With them were the special covenants made, to them was the law given, to them, worship was revealed and God's own promises announced. To them belong the Patriarchs, and as far as His natural descent was concerned, from them is the Christ, who is exalted and supreme over all, God, blessed forever! Amen!"

So, what could then be the problem of this people, with all these great privileges? Why is Paul crying for their salvation, what are they to be saved from? The answer brethren is IGNORANCE. Let us get back to Chapter 10: 2, 3, and confirm this, Paul continued the prayer; "for I bear them record, that they have a zeal of God but not according to (true, revelation) knowledge.

For being ignorant of God's righteousness, have not submitted themselves unto the righteousness of God". Incredible story! How can a people live in the midst of an ocean, yet wash their hands with spittle?

I have wondered for so many years of my Christian faith, how it could be said that God's own people (the Israelites) do not have the knowledge of God; with all the dealings they had with God through the wilderness; continual worship in the temples and synagogues; ready to kill anybody that blasphemes God's name in their religious fanaticism. Unfortunately, here we see God lamenting again through this revelation that we are sitting comfortably today where they all sat, to our own detriment.

What do I mean? When the Lord was through with the illustration He gave me, demonstrating the NEPA-LIGHT, as revealed in this dream, the Lord said, this is the same kind or level of knowledge that my people Israel lived on - general knowledge. In other words, we are still holding unto the same error today. This is further proof that the controversial situation that existed between God and men which prompted His crying out against His people in Hosea 4:1, 6 still exists today. The Lord is crying out again that there is no knowledge of God in the land, and therefore His people are perishing. God is sadly taking up the same lamentation against our generation. Very sad indeed!

Have you not wondered that our Lord Jesus Christ suffered humiliation, betrayal, persecution and finally the gruesome death under the hands of the religious leaders of His time? Today, is it not a common sight as God's undiluted Word {the only truth) is being played down by comedians and worldly philosophers on pulpits posing as preachers. We are suffering persecution today under the hands of our numerous, modernized, gospel preachers.

ILLUSTRATION OF THE NEPA LIGHT

The Lord gave a very clear illustration demonstrating the interpretation He gave for NEPA LIGHT. Remember the NEPA LIGHT represented all forms of general knowledge of God acquired from all known common sources. Using the secular, academic school curriculum existing as at the time of writing this book, the Lord went further to explain this revelation with the following illustration:

1. **At the Primary Education level:** The Lord reminded me that at primary school, we did a subject titled 'general knowledge'. This subject was made up of many subjects such as civics, primary science, geography, history, social science, etc. You discover that each of these sub-subjects making up the general knowledge constitutes a very wide field of knowledge. The higher we go in secular education, the more we narrow down to each of the subjects respectively, as chosen disciplines. It will therefore be foolish for anybody who stopped at this primary, 'general knowledge' level to claim that he or she knows civics, primary science or any of those subjects. This is just the same situation with those Christians who depend solely on the 'general knowledge of God's level (the NEPA LIGHT). How far can any Christian go with that primary level of God's knowledge?

2. **At the Post Primary Education Level:** The Lord also reminded me that we took a subject in the secondary school titled 'Integrated Science'. Under this subject we have branches of sciences namely – physics, chemistry and biology. Again, each of these branches of subjects opens up to become a field of learning as we

study further. The integrated science gets disintegrated into disciplines for detailed understanding of the subjects. Therefore, you will be fooling yourself to claim to have mastered any branch of these sub-subjects simply because you took integrated science at the first stage of your post primary school level. The integrated science subject knowledge acquired here is an example of NEPA LIGHT as revealed in the dream. I hope we are following the illustrations.

3. **At the University Education Level:** The Father took my memories again into the University degree programme. He reminded me about some courses that are referred to as General Studies (GS), mostly taken at the first and/or second year at the University. Irrespective of the discipline you have come to the University to pursue, you must study and pass GS 101 and the like. If you must be a graduate in whatever discipline, no matter the institution, you must pass 'General Studies'. If you enter the University and get carried away at the excitement of an excellent pass in General Studies (GS) courses, and end up not doing well in your major discipline (course of study), you are a complete failure. General Studies is mere basic knowledge meant to

broaden our understanding, to keep us balanced and give us a better flow commensurate with that level of learning. They may have very little input on our major courses of study, but we need them for a good take-off in pursuance of our majors. So, the GS course is another good example of the NEPA LIGHT, as revealed by the Father in the dream.

Are you getting a better understanding of this mystery? We can quickly discover and appreciate the Father's heart cry from these illustrations. As relevant and impacting as the General knowledge, integrated science and General studies are at those various levels of learning, they constitute only an infinitesimal part of the respective fields of learning which they are meant to introduce. There is a limit to which we can go with such knowledge. Even so is the NEPA LIGHT, as seen in the dream. No wonder all who depended on it were frustrated. The whole situation was hopeless. I marveled at the wisdom of God in making these illustrations.

Oh, my Brethren! We are inexcusable. At this point as the Father kept speaking, I felt like crying out from a mountain top about how unfair we have been to ourselves and to our God. You now discover that our God is more willing to share and reveal deeper things (secrets) of the Kingdom with us than we are willing or open to accommodate and get acquainted with. Elder James observed the same and admonished us in chapter 1:5 to go to God and ask for wisdom, because He giveth to all men liberally, and witholdeth not. But if you permit my candid opinion, the obvious sights around us leave us with no evidence of the fact that we (today's Christians) are tapping into this liberality.

OTHER INTERPRETATIONS

THE GENERATING SET AND LIGHT: Just as NEPA represented all man-made or common sources of power supply in the dream, the generating set stands for a personal source of power supply. Those that owned generating-sets in the dream were few, but very happy and relaxed. They felt relieved from the tension, depression and hopelessness that loomed as a result of the unreliable, erratic power supply. The power or light supplied by the generating set was their source of joy, as it provided succour for just the owner and their immediate family.

Interpreting the meaning of the generating set, the Lord said that it represented the source or the engine room of personal revelation knowledge of God. The same way NEPA stood for all known sources of general knowledge of God as explained earlier, the generating set supplies personal knowledge (light). The gen-set represents every personal device that provides the believer the opportunity of having a verbal discussion and a heart to heart impartation of revelation knowledge of God. A perfect example of such personal devices is the **'covenant time'** spent under the tutorship of the Holy Spirit alone in God's presence. I testified to you a little about the efficacy of the Covenant time in Chapter Two.

The Covenant Time is the generating set that brought me into the personal revelation realm of the knowledge of God which myself and my family are enjoying till today. This book is just one product made possible using my 'Spiritual Generating Set'. It is better experienced than told. It is a must for every believer. Unprecedented miracles and healings have been recorded just by resting in God's presence at Covenant Times. Like I said earlier, if you don't know about this move yet, or you don't know how to commence or you think you need more information for an optimal result, you should get in touch fast. This is an end time move, and cuts across denominational, racial, religious and other self/human created barriers. I wish you can drop all that pride and call now.

Other examples of this spiritual generating set are:

- Quality and consistent personal quiet time
- Quality and consistent personal altar Time
- Quality and consistent meditation time
- Other times spent alone with God not on prayer and warfare, but sitting down quietly alone with God and listening to the Master-Teacher.

NOTE: The implications of all these revelations and the accompanying lessons were all given to me by the Father. The subsequent chapters will expose their relevance to the minutest detail. It was however, at the point of explaining to me the importance of the generating set that my memory was awakened to this book title – 'KNOWING God PERSONALLY'. He said, it is only by making use of the generating set (personal light-supplier) that anybody can access Heaven's divine secrets. This is the only device by which men can know God personally. The generating set's personal light supplied stands for the highly needed personal illumination that will drive away the darkness occasioned by the unreliable NEPA LIGHT. This is the personal revelation knowledge that keeps you going when everywhere else is dark and dreary. Remember that light stands for the knowledge of the Word.

Men and Brethren! You will recall that I said earlier that this book title was given to me in the year 2003, while this revelation that brought the knowledge and inspiration to write it came three years after. Why the long gap? The truth is that nothing else, not my nearly three decades of Christian life and experience, nor any level of theological acquaintance qualifies me to do this work. Nothing could have made this work possible if not that I was one of the few that owned a generating set in that dream. It was God's grace, yet not cheap. Of course, you know, it will take some sacrifices to acquire a generating set, you must be tired of the darkness occasioned by the epileptic and unreliable NEPA LIGHT before you can be spurred on to look for a generator. This represents the extra sacrifice you must make to consistently stay in God's presence daily. Everything revealed in this dream, all have their spiritual implications as we will be discovering later.

As good and important as this spiritual – NEPA remained, we all need the SPIRITUAL GENERATING SET because NEPA was doing her best as revealed, but her impact on the society left great room to be desired. Our Lord Jesus said in Matt 11:27, 29: "All things are delivered unto me of my Father: and no man knows the Son but the Father, neither knows any man the Father, save the Son, and he to whomsoever the Son will reveal Him". How? Jesus added, "Learn of me… And you shall find rest unto your soul". Those that owned the generating set found rest in the midst of all the confusion and dissatisfaction. God is simply too much. I fear Him. Read more of the mysteries in this revelation in the chapters that follow and marvel at the wisdom of the Father.

5
THE KNOWLEDGE

Every dream, vision or revelation must be subjected to the screening test of the perfect law of liberty (the Holy Scriptures) before acceptance. If it is from the father, it must be in agreement with the written Word of God.

So, as the Father unveiled the lessons, packaged in this dream, He took me through the scriptures confirming the dream as a fulfillment of an end-time prophecy. The Lord gave me practical examples of some men and women that walked and worked with Him, and those that worked but walked in iniquity (Matt 7:21-23). The two groups of Christians all walked according to the knowledge of God they possessed, yet their activities and results were different. Why? The type or level of knowledge they had about God made the difference.

So many operated solely on NEPA-LIGHT, while some added the Genset to ensure consistent burning. So many people know about God, but few people know Him personally. So many stopped on the peripheral level of the knowledge of the Father, while a few made extra sacrifices to dig deeper to discover kingdom secrets. I am sure your life is about to experience an automatic turn round from the general, peripheral, unsustaining knowledge level to begin to seek to know and relate with the Father personally on an intimate level, as you take the contents of this book serious.

FULFILMENT OF PROPHECY

Brethren, the God we are serving is so thorough. His ways are past finding out. As the Lord led me from one level or branch to another of what I thought was a casual and insignificant dream, I could not stop wondering at His awesomeness. While wondering at the wisdom of God, He led me to the words of Hannah who declared "…let not arrogance come of man's mouth: for the Lord is a God of knowledge…" (1 Sam 2:3). Wow! When Hannah went into the realm of revelations, she discovered that most times, man speaks and acts from outside the realm of true knowledge, yet he speaks as if he is so certain about what he says, including Eli – the High Priest. Hannah said, this is man's arrogance. When we begin to operate from the realm of revelations, Christianity will know an unprecedented revival, because we will be overwhelmed by the knowledge of His will. We will discover that the time we are living in is very relevant and paramount in God's end-time programme, many prophecies are being fulfilled before us, yet none is laying it to heart. Where is your Bible?

So, the Lord took me to Isa 59:9-16 and chapter 60: 1-5, where I discovered that every word of this prophecy is being fulfilled in our time as demonstrated in this dream. The revelation insight given by the Lord as He interpreted the objects of the dream all fit into the words of this prophecy. You may need to study the two chapters above from the beginning to the end, because they are all relevant. I had to pick those few verses to avoid filling up the book with Bible texts which you can easily read from your Bible. So, we take it from vs 9 – Amplified Version. Please read through with understanding:

"Therefore, are justice and right far from us; and righteousness and salvation do not overtake us. We expectantly wait for light, but (only) see darkness, for brightness, but we walk in obscurity and gloom. We grope for the wall like the blind. Yes, we grope like those who have no eyes. We stumble at noonday as in the twilight; in dark places and among those who are full of life and vigor, we are as dead men… we look for justice, but there is none, for salvation, but it is far from us…. Rebelling against and denying the Lord, turning away from our God…and moaning from the heart words of falsehood. Justice is turned away backward, and righteousness (uprightness and right standing with God) stands far off; for truth has fallen in the street (the City's forum) and uprightness cannot enter (the courts of justice). Yes, truth is lacking…and the Lord saw it and it displeased Him that there was no justice. And He saw that there was no man and wondered that there was no intercessor (no one to intervene on behalf of truth and right): therefore His own arm brought Him victory and His own righteousness sustained Him".

This first segment of the prophecy refers to the NEPA-LIGHT situation and the associated problems of irregularity and the associated frustration as seen in the dream. We will be discussing more of this NEPA-LIGHT situation as presented in the first segment in this chapter text, while the second part of the prophecy refers to the Genset situation. All the lessons are very outstanding. We will consider this second part of personal, intimacy knowledge as presented in the next chapter.

A SEASON OF WANED EXPECTATIONS

I do not know your feelings but I am sure that anyone with a true sense of judgment will agree with me that the sights we see daily can best be described in these words of prophet Isaiah. It is indeed a season of waned expectation of everything, but darkness and gloom. We will consider the prophecy bit by bit to see how it is being fulfilled today in line with this revelation of God.

JUSTICE, RIGHTEOUSNESS AND SALVATION IS FAR FROM US

The dream revealed a waned expectation of light and everything it stood for. Righteousness, equity, transparency, and justice are obvious manifestations of light and sound knowledge of God. Unfortunately, you will agree with me that this is a far cry from our society today. How can there be justice and righteousness in a season when men lack knowledge of the way of peace but devised crooked paths? This was the problem stated in vs 8 of our text which is the fountain of those ugly sights from vs 9. We see no fear of God in men of our generation. Righteousness and justice are products of a personally disciplined lifestyle which can only be made possible by a personal knowledge of the terribleness of God the Father in dealing with men of a contrary lifestyle (Rom. 2:11). Nobody sleeps and wakes up into such a glorious lifestyle.

You are all witnesses! How many times have you taken a matter to the Pastor, Bishop, G.O, elders or church committee, expecting some justice and fairness, but came back battered and disappointed? Clearly, you watched everybody dance and trifle with the truth, being overwhelmed by prejudice and favouritism. If you do not belong to a certain class and do not have enough money to pay for justice in our society today, you are finished. What is the reason? Shallow knowledge of God the Father! If you have not experienced this ungodly victimization, I believe you can name one or two victims of denied justice around you.

Today, because justice cannot be gotten within the court of the saints (call it the church), we now take our matters to the courts of the unjust. Is this not common with us? Ministers taking one another to the law courts, members against members, ministers against members and vice versa. Will you say these men and women don't know God? Of course, they know so much about Him, but not beyond the general knowledge level. You hear them quote scriptures profusely to defend their actions.

Let us sincerely consider the following ministration of Paul the apostle and compare it with how the church is acting today in relating to one another. Many of us have preached from there. Oh! But it does not seem applicable to the church today. Listen to Brother Paul: "Dare any of you, having a matter against another go to law before the unjust, and not before saints? Do you not know that the saints shall judge the world? And if the world shall be judged by you, are you unworthy to judge the smallest matters? Know ye not that we shall judge angels? How much more things that pertain to this life... I speak this to your shame (if we still retain some sense of shameful feelings). Is it so, that there is not a wise man among you? No, not one that shall be able to judge between his brethren? But brother goeth to law with brother and that before the unbelievers... why do ye not rather take wrong? Why do ye not rather suffer yourselves to be defrauded...?" (I Cor 6).

Brethren, is it at this level of our knowledge of God that we will stand fit to judge the angels? See how justice, equity and righteousness have taken flight from the supposed custodians and executors of the same. 'Allow myself to be defrauded? No way! That must be an archaic and obsolete gospel'. That has been our disposition. SELF is the problem. It will take a man who lives beyond the general knowledge level (the level where the Corinthian Church operated then) to escape the gallows of 'MR. SELF' in our time. That grace is only made available when we spend time ALONE IN GOD'S PRESENCE. Look at the prophecy again.

DARKNESS IN PLACE OF LIGHT

"...we wait expectantly for light but only see darkness, for brightness, but we walk in obscurity... we grope for the wall like the blind, we stumble at noonday..."

Remember the dream; how people waited endlessly for light, but it came only in trickles not enough to brighten peoples' lives and environment. We also saw people hopelessly wallowing in obscurity. The situation the Lord presented in the dream is perfectly demonstrating the fulfillment of this prophecy of Isaiah in our time. But we are not mindful of this.

Remember also, the interpretations the Lord gave concerning the light. This prophecy cannot be referring to physical light and darkness, hence it was said that people stumbled at noonday. The situation prescribed here is worse than physical darkness predicament. When people grope for the wall like the blind and stumble at noonday, then it suggests that there is everything wrong with that kind of light. It is not illuminating enough to guide people's steps. This is where we have found ourselves in this generation; in a very sorry state! Too much knowledge about God, yet we remain destitute of God's righteousness, aliens to every kingdom secret and going about establishing our own righteousness.

Remember again, the words of the Psalmist which the Lord used in explaining what light represented in this dream. "The entrance of your word giveth light"; "Thy word is a lamp unto my feet and a light unto my path" (Ps 119:130,105). What does this suggest in line with this prophecy? The implication of all this is that through the knowledge of God's Word, the illuminating power seems to fill our land, yet lacks the potency to illuminate our path and guide our feet. Having eyes wide open but lacking sight and perception. Why? Because the potency of the Word to provide illumination lies beyond mere letters. The result is that we keep groping for the wall like the blind, and stumble at noonday. Then, something must be seriously wrong with such a level of knowledge. Such knowledge is void of potency!

The Father is here and is now revealing this secret to us, that He is deeper than we see on the surface. The general knowledge level at which most of us stops cannot grant us access into divine secrets that must guide our feet daily to and through the Father's will for our personal lives. This was the position where Paul met the children of Israel (his kinsmen) that prompted his continued sorrowing for them in Rom 9:1-5; and 10:1-3. Very unfortunate situation! We are bathing in the midst of a pool of water, yet soap is entering our eyes. The children of Israel have suffered terrible humiliations as a result of this careless disposition to the Word of life.

History is repeating itself brethren! So sadly! "For the things that were written aforetime are written for our learning" (Rom 15:4). The Father is calling out to us again through this revelation, to leave this commoners' level and come into a place of ultimate, personal communion with Him. You need the Gen-set! Wake up! Back to the prophecy again.

DEAD MEN AMONG THE LIVING

"...in the dark places and among those who are full of life and vigour, we are as dead men."

THE KNOWLEDGE

What a sight to behold brethren! God has always left for Himself a remnant. Isn't it wonderful that in the midst of the darkness, the general decadence and depression, some people were seen to be full of life and vigour. Remember the dream again: while majority of the people were hopelessly cast down and dejected because the power supply was so bad that it could hardly sustain any life, a few were confident and relaxed, because they possessed the Gen-set. Who are these blessed few? Find out more in the next Chapter.

Meanwhile, in the midst of a people full of life and vigour, so many remained as dead men. May you not be found among this latter group! Yet, this is the obvious condition in our present-day Christian settings. So many professors of divine knowledge, yet in every good work, we are found wanting. Who are these dead men, yet living among people full of life and vigour? The word 'among' would suggest that they all stood under the same platform. They all had the same divine opportunities, the same access into God's manifold grace, under the same supply of NEPA – sources, having the same freedom to either choose to settle on the peripheral knowledge level or dig deeper and knock harder to personally access kingdom secrets, and all other common grounds. Oh. The scripture cannot be broken, "For the grace of God that bringeth salvation hath appeared to all men, teaching us that denying ungodliness and worldly lusts, we should (be able to live) live soberly, righteously and godly, in this present world" (Titus 2:11,12).

If the grace is made available to all men, what then is responsible for such a great divide: while some were fully alive, some were completely on the opposite side? Think about it. It becomes very clear that neither God nor destiny can be faulted in this matter. Nothing else could have been responsible than the difference in choices made by individuals. They were not willing to take the extra sacrifice to stay and learn IN HIS PRESENCE to make up for the shortfalls of the General Christian knowledge level.

Their words betray them. You can easily identify the dead men from their words: "Believe it or not, I am a Christian; even if I end up a gateman in heaven, I have tried; once I am born again, God no longer reckons sin to me; I will remain a Christian, it doesn't matter what

I do after salvation; God is full of mercy, so I can't go to hell fire" and many of such self-defensive statements you know. These are dead men among the living. Where do you stand qualified?

Their actions betray them. You can also identify them by their actions, dead men among the living. They can quote all the promises of God in the scriptures but know nothing and do nothing about the 'IF Conditions' attached to the promises. Like Esau, every cry of the flesh must be satisfied at the expense of their eternal birth right. After all, 'they can eat their cake and have it over and over'. Dead men! Such is their disposition... Listen to Esau: "Behold, I am at the point to die; and what profit shall this birthright do to me" (Gen 25:29-34).

In the face of every trial, all they see and confess is death and no life. They graduate from one level of mistake, into a more complex one, because they can never own up to their mistakes. Of course, so much grace is required to be able to be disciplined enough to own up to a self-induced error. That level of grace to be able to own up to our weaknesses or failures, and make amends can only be received in God's presence. These men are not ready for that extra mile. After satisfying the flesh, Esau hated his brother Jacob and started planning to slay him (Gen.27:41). What a life? The same way Cain went. Among people full of life and vigour, they always chose the way of death.

Dead men among the living are all around us. They are easy to be recognized: They know so much and make the loudest noise about God's mercies but know little or nothing about His terrible consuming wrath. Their complete dependence upon NEPA sources, and acquaintance with only the general knowledge of God makes them friends of every 'notable' minister or prophet that comes to town. They can flow with Moses for a while, as long as they are seeing him. When Moses is not there, they can easily prevail on the available, flexible pastor Aaron to make them a god, because they have no personal faith (Exd.32:1). Incredible, inconsistent folks.

The next time, you will find them among the team of Korah, Dathan and Abiram (Numb 16). They hear from every prophet in town about God's will and plan for their own lives. They can be anywhere, but their Fathers' inner court. What a people! Do you blame them? The only knowledge they have about God their Father is the one people taught them. They don't have any personal altar where their Father talks to them daily. What a generation!

This attitude was responsible for the great demise suffered by the wicked servant in one of the parables of our Lord Jesus Christ (Luke 19:11-27), demonstrating the Father's walking and working relationship with His servants. If we don't know Him personally, we cannot walk with Him; if we cannot walk with Him, we cannot work with Him. In this parable, a certain noble man who was traveling to a far country to receive a kingdom for himself and come back called his servants and gave one pound to each of them to do business and to occupy (take full charge of his business) till he comes. Incidentally, the citizens of the land held various unwholesome opinions about this noble man and did everything to stop his coming back, but they could not. He wielded so much power and authority. When the noble man returned with great exploits, it was a great moment of excitement for some of His servants and great disappointment for some. What was the cause of this great divide? Dead men among those full of life and vigour manifested again. The servants that had intimate knowledge of their master treasured Him so much, and were fully persuaded that public opinion will not stop his coming back. The wicked servant never knew his master all along. So, he was overtaken by the public opinion of the citizens in vs 14. Look at his account in vs 20 and 21 "...Lord, behold here is thy pound, which I have kept laid up in a napkin: For I feared thee, because thou art an austere man; thou takest up that thou layest not down, and reapest that thou didst not sow".

What was his evidence? How did he suddenly come about this opinion about his master? He believed the public opinion about his own master. If he knew all these about his master, was he not foolish to remain a servant under such a master? You know the rest of the story. Of course, he paid so dearly for this ignorance. Of course, wrong knowledge would always produce wrong result. Remember, the noble man in this parable represents our Lord Jesus Christ, while these servants here represent you and myself. It will be wisdom to sincerely check out where you fit in among these servants! How much do you know the master you call your Lord? Think seriously about this. The wicked servant got worse than he bargained for.

THE KORAH TEAM:

Now look at this, "Korah…, Dathan and Abiram… and On, sons of Reuben took men; (anybody can take them and use them, because they are like dead men). And they rose up before Moses, with certain of the children of Israel, two hundred and fifty princes of the assembly, famous in the congregation, men of renown; and they gathered themselves together against Moses and Aaron…" (Num 16:1-3). They are easily attracted to fame, crowds and whatever is happening; it does not matter to them if the happenings are in the Father's will or not. What attracts them is the noise of the event and not the legitimacy of the event, not the relevance of the event, not the eternal value of the event. They are easy to be recognized! You can easily find them in the company of those who claim 'we all know God', and never among those who 'know their God'. They follow the crowd to any destination, not asking any question.

TEN DEAD VERSUS TWO LIVING

When the ten spies divided themselves against Joshua and Caleb bringing an evil, faithless report, the dead men among the wilderness church all melted, not knowing their God, personally. Hear them out: "We be not able to go up against the people; for they are stronger than we… The land through which we have gone to search it, is a land that eateth up its inhabitants, and are men of great stature,… and we were in our own sight as grasshoppers" (Num 13:31-33). Compare this with the earlier persuasive report of Caleb and Joshua in vs 30. "And Caleb stilled the people before Moses saying, let us go up at once, and possess it, for we are well able to overcome it".

The choice of word 'overcome' indicates that Joshua and Caleb knew there was going to be a battle before the possession, but they have also known personally that their God never loses any battle. These are men full of life and vigour. How much do you know about the God you claim to be serving? "For the just shall live by His faith" (Hab 2:4). Faith, as we know is a product of knowledge (Rom 10:17). Therefore, common knowledge will produce common faith while personal, intimate knowledge will definitely produce personal, unwavering faith.

The Bible added in Num 14:1 that after hearing the two opposing reports, the people made their choice as usual in which camp to pitch their tent. Once again, the dead among the living stood out. Child of God do everything not to be numbered among the dead, in the midst of all opportunities to be identified with the living. Being found in the company of the dead has great consequences.

DANGEROUS CONSEQUENCIES

"And all the congregation lifted up their voice, and cried and the people wept that night". The end result was disastrous. They murmured against God, Moses and Aaron and brought great damnation upon themselves, for the Lord spoke: "As truly as I live, saith the Lord, as ye have spoken in mine ears, so will I do to you. Your carcasses shall fall in this wilderness… from twenty years upwards which have murmured against me… But your little ones, which ye said should be prey, them will I bring in, and they shall know the land which ye have despised… And those men that did bring up the evil report upon the land, died by the plague before the Lord... But Joshua ... and Caleb... which were of the men that went to search the land, lived still" (Num 14:28-38). What a tragic end for many, while few (who knew their God intimately) lived still. They made the choice!

Brethren, it is dangerous to hang all your faith upon the best of teachings and stories about the God of heaven and earth. Rather, seek further to know Him personally and experientially. How much you know Him determines your flow in spiritual matters ultimately now and where you end up. The team of Korah, Dathan and Abiram ended up the same way: the earth opened her mouth and swallowed them up... all the men that appertained unto Korah, and all their goods (Num 16:32). The previous day, their voices went high against Moses, as if they knew the Lord better than Moses, and as if they spoke from the Lord's side, but next day they met their waterloo.

THEY LOVE TEMPORARY PLEASURES, NOT KNOWING ETERNAL VALUES

It is dangerous to relate with the Father from a distance,

because you will never get to know Him from there. When Ahithophel served David, he was noted for his wise counsel; "...as if a man inquired at the oracle of God (2 Sam16:23). That was the testimony of Ahithophel while he worked with David. I am sure he must have learnt this from David who often resorted to God and inquired in His temple (Ps.27:4). So, it worked for him until he suddenly lost touch with the secret place and joined the commoners in the field pursing 'wealth and games'. Ahithophel joined the camp of Absalom to rebel against David. Knowing his Father intimately even in the face of his hard trials, David prayed this simple prayer: "O Lord, I pray thee, turn the counsel of Ahithophel into foolishness (2 Sam 15: 31). The result was that for the first time, Ahithophel's counsel was rejected, "And Ahithophel saw that his counsel was not followed, he got to his house and put his household in order, and hanged himself and died..." (2 Sam 17:23). Don't leave the place of His presence! It is the personal Gen-set that divinely empowers you when NEPA is failing.

The sons of the prophets at Bethel, another set of trainee prophets at Jericho, and another band of fifty of the sons of the prophets all stood on the same platform with Elisha to tap into the secrets that made Elijah an outstanding prophet. They all had the opportunity to do great exploits. But they chose to remain on the common, general knowledge of God level. The Bible recorded that '… they stood to view (Elijah and Elisha) afar off…' (2 Kings 1:3, 5, 7). They remained afar off while Elisha went far in to possess a double portion of Elijah's anointing. The farther you are from the place of intimate, personal fellowship with the Father, the closer you are to the place of the multitude, that is, those who dwell on 'The general knowledge level'. You cannot access heaven's secrets from that distance. The closer you are to the world, the farther you are from God.

Gehazi, the servant of Elisha was another privileged child of God, but he missed the place of 'HIS PRESENCE'. He preferred to remain on the peripheral knowledge level, enjoying the mercies and coverings of the calling, but not ready for any in-depth walk with the Master. While Elisha had great fun in God's presence before daybreak, Gehazi was different. Look at his style: "And when the servant of the man of God (Gehazi) was risen early, and gone forth, behold, a host compassed the city both with horses and chariots, and he cried out, Alas my master! How shall we do? (2 Kgs 6:15). How can we know what to do at crisis point, when all we do is wake up early and hit the road? No personal altar; no place of personal intercourse with our Bridegroom. What a careless bride we are!

Total dependence on NEPA-supplied light can be dangerous. Even when our Bishops, Pastors, Parents and all that constitute our NEPA-sources are doing their very best effectively, we all need this personal intimate closer walk with the Master, else we will never get to know Him passionately well. It is this personal aspect of the knowledge that keeps us going at crisis times. It is not a good Christian virtue to always run to the pastor for answers to every little shaking you have in this Christian journey. You must work out your own (personal) salvation (Phil 2:12).

This is getting yourself the spiritual gen-set. At the time of crisis and emergencies, temptations and trials of faith which are inevitable in this Christian journey, we need the personal knowledge of God to survive them. Seek to know God personally. So, Gehazi could not take advantage of serving Elisha to seek to inherit a double portion of his master's anointing (as Elisha did), rather he inherited Naaman's leprosy (2 Kgs 5:27). What a great 'achievement'!

I can go on and on to give us examples of people that lived as dead men, among men full of life and vigour. Their end has always been disastrous. My fear is that history is about to repeat itself, a very bad history for that matter! May we take heed!

TRUTH BY MAJORITY

"...for truth has fallen in the street (the city's forum), and uprightness cannot enter (the courts of justice). Yes, truth is lacking..."

May the Lord save our generation. The church of Jesus Christ was founded on truth. It is the "pillar and ground of the truth" (1 Tim 3:15). But today, truth is fallen in the street. Truth is now determined in the city's forum; by 'majority carries the vote'. It does not matter if the minority holds the real truth. How and where can we find truth these days when nobody is willing to pay the price to receive revelation knowledge of the truth from the One and only source? (Jn 14:6).

Truth determined by public opinion or in the mouth of two or three witnesses could be dangerous. It has caused a lot of problems. Many have gathered together to raise false witnesses against the innocent. The Pharisees nailed our Lord Jesus Christ 'at the testimony of two or three witnesses' just as the law prescribed. Yet all their accusations against Jesus were false. Truth determined by the decision of the committee of elders, prophets or bishops outside the revelation of God have brought about great conflicts in today's church. Most times it doesn't matter to us if those committees are the same type of group of four hundred prophets that spoke in one voice against the lonely voice of Micaiah in 1 Kgs 22:2. They all chorused to Jehoshaphat and the king of Israel, "… Go up to Ramoth-Gilead and prosper, for the Lord shall deliver it into the King's hand" but the same King of Israel went to Ramoth-Gilead and died, according to the minority voice of Micaiah (truth in minority).

Brethren, which type of truth are we holding unto

today? How did we arrive at what we are teaching and practicing? Is it founded on the Apostolic, undiluted doctrine? Is it born out of revelation knowledge or copied from other churches or people? As long as the majority of the churches or 'Christians' are doing it or preaching it, it cannot be wrong. Who told us those lies? What a way to determine the truth! What truth are you thriving on today? Please care enough to know. The great doctors and learned priests (Nicodemuses) that were astonished at the revelation knowledge of Jesus have become the experts of our time in our churches (Luk 2:46, 47 and Jn 3:1-9). Why? Because we are all hanging and operating on the same level – 'general Christian knowledge' (NEPA-LIGHT)! We need the gen-set else we get swallowed up by the majority force that cares nothing about the truth.

6
THE CONFIRMATION

While I was putting this work together, the Lord gave a woman a dream and sent her to me. She never knew I was working on this book project and of course, I never discussed it with her till the publication of the book. She came and narrated the revelation she had to me simply because I was one of those she saw playing a very prominent role in that revelation, she did not know that the Lord sent her to bring a confirmation to the message He is bringing us in this book.

THE CONFIRMING REVELATION

The woman narrated her dream as follows: In a dream she found herself and every member of the church all seated in a normal Sunday service. All the pastors in our church then and the members were all in the fellowship. One of the pastors ministered to the congregation, while we all sat down and listened. Among the pastors that were seated and listening was this woman and myself. We all sat in the front row opposite the ministering pastor.

As the preaching was going on, God opened her eyes in that dream, and she saw the heavens were opened. She saw that God was speaking to the preacher - pastor, and was expecting him to transmit the messages to the listening audience. To her greatest amazement, she discovered that this preacher was absolutely on his own. He was not paying any attention to the voice of God coming from on high. The preacher was not hearing the voice of God at all. Meanwhile, he was busy charismatically saying his own mind, far from what the Lord was echoing from the heavens.

When she looked at the other ministers seated, she discovered that I was worried and seriously disturbed where I was seated. Why? She wondered! She then observed that I was also hearing the Lord speaking to the preacher, while the preacher was saying something else to the church. She saw me almost trying to use signals to draw the attention of the preacher to listen to what God was saying and preach the same, but he never got the signals. She said she heard me saying, "Why can't this pastor hear what the Lord is saying; why is he saying a different thing altogether?" She saw me in that worried mood, and she woke up.

When she finished sharing this revelation with me, she added a word of advice that I should try and be patient with other ministers that seem not to be catching up fast in ministering the word. "Hm-mm," I sobbed. I knew that this was the least important aspect of the messages the Lord was revealing through this dream. I was not the General Overseer of the church, neither do I have those ministers under my control. So, what is my business with being patient with those other ministers? I do not have direct control or authority over any of them. However, as I left her and looked up to the Lord to expose to me the lesson[s] in this dream, He turned my memory to this book in your hands. Marvelous God! So, putting together other dealings of the Lord with me in this end time, I understood perfectly what the Lord was saying through this dream, it came as a confirmation to the core message of this book.

CONFIRMATION LESSONS

When I meditated over the dream of this woman sent to me by God, here is a list of the lessons that became clear in this confirming revelation as illuminated by the Holy Spirit for a better understanding of what the Spirit is saying to the church.

The first lesson here is that this pastor was meant to be standing and ministering as an oracle of God, but according to the revelation he was completely disconnected from the Spirit-source. His spiritual ears were so dead and deaf that he couldn't hear God speaking. So, what was all that he was preaching? Your guess is as good as mine. He preached from his head knowledge about whatever subject he was speaking on. He spoke from the NEPA-LIGHT general knowledge. He preached only from the letters (written words, logos) that kills, because he lacked the current to tap into the spoken words (rhema) from above.

The second lesson here is that this is the common scenario of most of our fellowship activities today. So, we only gather religiously and go back the same way we came. No life is affected or touched spiritually because we are never in touch with and in tune with God .

Another lesson here is that every fellowship activity is made up of two different types of audience. We have those that came just as other participants, having no specific expectation. We also have those who come with great expectations. They come determined to worship God and receive divine impartations. We can easily discover the two types of audience by their attitudes. The unserious, non-expectant ones do all the dancing, yield easily to all the emotional excitements and grab whatever comes from the pulpit as literally as it comes. Most of them end up as pastor's converts and fans and not God's. Unfortunately, it was very clear from this revelation that the 'general knowledge' set of audience are always the majority. They all sat down and listened because they never knew that the preacher was disconnected from God.

The second set of church audiences are those who do not depend solely on church activities for their spiritual growth. These are the Gen set possessors, who do not compromise with their daily devotional, personal relationship with the Lord. Most times they already receive ahead of time from their personal altar, a spiritual revelation of what the Lord has prepared to feed His church on each fellowship day. If you are a devout Christian reading this book, you will testify that this is a common experience. So, this set of audience knows when the preacher is delivering the message fresh from the altar, and when he is out of tune and time with God. This set were represented in this revelation by the woman that had this dream and me. It becomes pertinent to ask yourself at this point, my dear reader which church audience do you belong to?

Other important, soul searching questions are as follows:
- What do you think about the great harm that is being done to the life and eternal destiny of the first set of church members? Though they are wonderful church members and pastors' praise singers, they cannot discern the Lord's voice.
- Don't you think that with this laissez-faire attitude to Christian living, you will have yourself to blame, and not the preachers, if you miss heaven? Isn't it obvious that the gate of heaven is opened so wide for 'whoever will' to relate with the Lord personally?

Summarily, it becomes very easy to understand from this confirming revelation that some will go to hell fire from the pew, and some will go to hell fire from the pulpit! What a great tragedy! Only, a personal knowledge of God will spare us from this time bomb. One serious matter that also calls for concern as revealed in this dream is the problem of scarcity of truth present in too many churches and religious organizations. What do I mean? The simple reason why truth remains scarce in the midst of growing religious activities is this disconnection between church leaders and preachers from the God of the church.

A VERY COSTLY DEATH

It is indeed a season when uprightness cannot enter the courts of justice. The result of such situation is gross lawlessness. This same kind of unpleasant situation loomed for a long season in Israel. "Now for a long season Israel hath been without the true God, and without a teaching priest, and without law," (2 Chron. 15:3). It therefore became a season of lawlessness, troubles, and great vexation (vs 4-5). Does this not practically describe our society today? Like the ostrich, we all bury our heads inside church activities as if we do not know that our society is a reflection of the church. Our society does not in any way suggest that our numerous church activities are yielding fruits. Does it not bother you? If only we can be sincere enough, we will agree with God. Too many priests, with all the accompanying titles, yet our generation knows little or nothing about the TRUE GOD.

They know so much about the little gods and demons because sixty percent of our preaching(s) is dedicated to the operations of demons. Why? Because such preaching gives us the opportunity to showcase how 'powerful' we are in dealing with the demons. How I wish we were really dealing with them. Long nights of vigils and weeks of fasting and prayers are being dedicated to deliverance from 'every cockroach that flies above our head' and to kill our 'enemy-suspects'. The next thirty percent of our ministrations are dedicated to preaching of miracles and prosperity without hard work; one million ways you can make money without diligently laying your hands on the plow; a thousand ways you can get your dream-life partner without essentially partnering with the Holy Spirit, and many more. The remaining ten percent is dedicated to psyching the people's emotions with many shouts of Hallelujah! Praise God! The Lord is good and all that, while using choice words to persuade men to give bountifully and receive a twenty four hour miracle. "If you give ten thousand naira now, you will receive one million in twenty four hours from now. Receive your miracle! Receive your breakthrough! And many such statements we are used to hearing.

Now tell me how anybody sitting under these kind of ministrations will learn the righteousness and holiness of God that produces uprightness in men? How do we become acquainted with other deeper matters of Kingdom life? Where will the uprightness come from without people coming to terms with God's mercies and severity (Rom 11:22)? So many Priests everywhere, yet there is a serious dearth of 'teaching priests' in our time. We can stand behind the podium preaching for hours without any trace of heaven or hell in our long sermons. Is this not the common experience? This was the sight demonstrated in the revelation – people looked up to NEPA, but NEPA wasn't coming forth with that kind of light generation that can advance the lives of men.

THE VEIL IS TORN APART

Men and brethren, we cannot afford to resign our eternal destiny to fate after the veil has been rolled away. The veil that once debarred men from accessing the Holiest of holies has been torn apart for whosoever wills to enter freely. Don't remain outside; where it is happening now is inside the Holiest of holies (Heb 10:19-22). Hear this: "And the Spirit and the bride say, come, and let him that heareth, say come. And let him that is athirst come. And whosoever will, let him take the water of life freely" (Rev 22:17). The Landlord-occupants of the Holiest of holies are the ones giving out the invitation to 'come'. In other words, the invitation is into the Holiest of Holies where the event is taking place. You can only meet them where they reside, else you cannot be said to have honoured this invitation. The Father, the Son, and the Holy Spirit inhabit the Holiest of Holies. We can make the most of this invitation, to access heaven's secrets on a daily basis. How? By keeping a daily covenant time in HIS PRESENCE.

No matter how wonderful our NEPA sources might be in giving the light, implying, no matter how charismatic, how skilled in oratory, prophetic and spiritually consistent our preachers might be, if we follow them with the utmost diligence (which is very impossible), we can end up with another duplicate of that preacher (leader). This is against God's plan for our lives. No man is created a duplicate of another man. We are all born to grow into the fullness of the image of Christ and not man. So, you must find out whose image you reflect. We can only grow into the true image of our Lord Jesus Christ as we sit daily in God's presence, "with open face beholding as in a glass the glory of the Lord; then we are changed into the same image (the Adamic image which was lost by Adam) from glory to glory, as by the Spirit of the Lord" (2 Cor 3:18).

So brethren, God knew that there will come such a time when teachers of the total gospel would be scarce, therefore "unto everyone of us is given grace according to the measure of the gift of Christ. Wherefore He saith, when He ascended up on high. He led captivity captive, and gave gifts (talents) unto men" (including you) Eph.4:7-8. We are all therefore responsible for whichever or at whatever level of knowledge we settle for concerning the mysteries of the Godhead and the eternal Kingdom.

Here we are brethren; end-time prophecies, meant to put us on alert in readiness for His appearing are being fulfilled in our time, but we don't seem to have been careful enough to observe the events. In verses 15 and 16 of Isa 59, the prophecy continued, "yes truth is lacking…and the Lord saw it, and it displeased Him that there was no justice. And He saw that there was no intercessor (no one to intervene on behalf of truth and right); therefore, His own arm brought Him victory, and His own righteousness sustained Him". What a costly death! What a solution induced by necessity.

YOU HAVE A CHOICE

This is no time to sit still in the church watching, as if helpless, all this erosion of the biblical ancient landmarks. This is no time to join them or follow the trend, not caring about the force behind the tide. Don't sit idle and watch our NEPA–sources, even when it is obvious you are being covered up with gross darkness. Our Father God did not create you to live at the mercy of any other being. Behave like your Father, if indeed you are one of His children. The young lion displays every attribute of her parent. You have no reason to keep groping for the wall; don't die in obscurity.

When the Lord saw the dirty situation, the decadence, and the carelessness of everybody towards the truth, He stirred up Himself; His own arm brought Him victory; His own righteousness sustained Him. What did it take Him? Sacrifice! You can get the Gen-set. Yes! You can: you need it for a steady, sustaining light, for better and brighter illumination, to guide your feet and your steps daily to become more like Jesus.

Therefore, the Lord charged in chapter 60:1 of Isaiah, as a result of all the facts we examined in chapter 59: "Arise, shine; for thy light is come and the glory of Lord is risen upon thee". This is the Gen-set – the personal grace to receive constant illumination is made available.

The mysteries will be revealed in the next chapter. Meanwhile, you cannot afford to stay a minute longer on the peripheral level of God's knowledge. You have scratched enough on the surface, and that is responsible for your rising and falling, lack of steady growth, no radiance of the revelation knowledge of the Father, no reflection of His Glory. Nobody comes into his Father's house and stands aloof, except of course a very bad son or daughter. I am sure we will not want to be identified as one, but our actions betray us.

A situation where what you know about your Father is secondhand information from your Papa, Reverend, Bishop, Pastor, Prophet, Evangelist and the likes is not healthy at all. Oh! They might be wonderful and very accurate in delivering their messages to you but those messages will remain only on the information level, until you personally set out time to sit down in His presence to personally meditate and digest them. It is at this point of meditation and Holy Spirit-led Discipleship hour (ALONE IN HIS PRESENCE) that the information will be broken down and personalized, producing the knowledge that will illuminate your hearts and work out God's purpose in you and for you. This is revelation knowledge.

We will talk more on the prophetic aspect of this mystery – 'The Gen-set supplied light' in the next chapter. But for now, you must establish where you stand. What level of knowledge have you been thriving on as a Christian? Dare to be sincere. You have a choice!

7

THE MYSTERY

So far, we have been drawing inference from the prophecy of Isaiah chapter 59 to buttress this prophetic mystery as the Lord unfolded it. I did encourage us in the chapter five of this book that you pause for a while and study the two chapters 59 and 60 of Isaiah fully to appreciate their relevance to this revelation. If you did, you will interestingly, discover that the very disappointing and hopeless situation expressed in chapter 59 suddenly opened up and gave way into a very exciting life in chapter sixty. It was such a turnaround from the gloomy, groping life in obscurity to a glorious, glowing life of the Gen-set, empowered, consistent light. What could have made this great difference in such a very short while?

THE MYSTERY LIES IN THE GEN-SET:

The switching over from sole dependence on NEPA-SOURCE to a very consistent source – THE GENEREATING-SET source for light made the difference. This is a mystery, but revealed to us by the Holy Spirit. We will discover it soon as the Father went further to interpret this dream with biblical illustrations. Meanwhile, let us consider some few verses from Isa 60: 1-5 (AMP). We will be taking it from the Amplified version to queue up perfectly from where we stopped in chapter five of this book.

"Arise. (From the depression and frustration in which circumstances have kept you – rise to a new life)! Shine (be radiant with the glory of the Lord), for your light has come, and the glory of the Lord has risen upon you! For behold, darkness shall cover the earth and dense (gross) darkness (all) people, but the Lord shall arise upon you, and His glory shall be seen on you. And nations shall come to your light and kings to the brightness of your rising. Lift up your eyes round about you and see! They all gather themselves together, they came to you. Your sons shall come from afar, and your daughters shall be carried and nursed in your arms. Then you shall see and be radiant, and your heart shall thrill and tremble with joy at the glorious deliverance) and be enlarged; because the abundant wealth of the sea shall be turned to you, unto you shall the nations come with their treasure".

ARISE AND SHINE

Brethren, in the midst of the gross darkness that covered the people; in the midst of the confusion and depression created by the unwholesome nature of the general light (the general knowledge of God's word), which is not illuminating enough to guide the people's daily steps, came this clarion call to "whosoever will" to ARISE AND SHINE. Isn't this wonderful?

Nobody is created or born into the kingdom to live at the mercy of any other person not even the devil. You are in the kingdom at a time like this for a specific purpose known to the Father alone. Unless you wake up from obscurity and begin to access Him that dwells in the midst of the cherubim, the eternal Father of all flesh, you will never get to discover your purpose for life. Every life – purpose is heaven born and heaven bound. Every life lived outside this purpose is worthless and wasted. Ask King Solomon, he calls it labouring for the wind (Ecc.5:16)? Each day or minute you spend outside this purpose is a time carelessly ceded to the devil to our own detriment.

What do you discover from here? You must spend time IN HIS PRESENCE daily to have God reveal to you His purpose per time, if you must live a meaningful and fulfilling life here. This is what people refer to as VISION – the propelling force of every successful man. VISION is a break-off or a branch of purpose. It is God's revealed purpose per time (Hab.2:3). When you catch it and run with it, you make a difference, a good success. This is what distinguishes the living from dead men. So, who wants to remain dead or live a life not guided by vision or purpose? Nobody would willingly opt for that, but what we see around us suggests otherwise.

Vision is not common. Nobody sleeps and suddenly wakes up into God's purpose for his/her life. It is a product of PERSONAL REVELATION KNOWLEDGE (Acts 26:13-20) which is available to those that possesses the Gen-set. ARISE! Get your Gen-set.

Don't settle for what you met on ground, nor live on secondhand information about the God you call your Father. Our God is not an object of worship; He is a great and real personality. In other words, He is not to you who they say He is, He is only who you say He is. It is who you understand Him to be that works for you and affects your daily walk (relationship) with Him. The best any other preacher can succeed in exposing you to about God can at best present Him as a great and terrible object of worship. This is very correct of course, but only presents one side of the coin. Christ came to take us far beyond this level, hence the prophetic cry – ARISE AND SHINE, because your light is come.

YOUR LIGHT IS COME

Oh my God, people sat still in that dream as if they could not afford the Gen-set but no, it was a matter of choice. I cannot reconcile the fact that I possessed a Gen-set in that dream to being financially buoyant, but because I could not just stand the frustration of just depending on NEPA-LIGHT.

What do we see today in our contemporary world of faith? People (Christians) gulp everything (every message) that comes with a Pentecostal tag. Every deviation receives a pass-mark for a new doctrine and becomes acceptable to all. Watch millions of people troop in and out of 'worship centres', singing only the praise of their musical entertainers and their 'man of God', knowing nothing about the God of the man of God. You hardly find the Godly reverence that attests to true worship among our numerous worshippers today. Who cares about the faith once delivered unto the saints (Jude 3).

To know God personally, you must choose to leave this peripheral level. Take advantage of your light that is already come. The Father never demands what He cannot provide. You will never know the joy of being a child of God until you get to know Him by revelation. The illumination that the knowledge of God's word brings is unprecedented; it dispels every darkness. Each new day, we wake up very ignorant of what the day holds for us and our families. It is dangerous to go through the day in such ignorance. We all wake up excitedly, but in ignorance of the Father's programme for our lives until we get to the altar to commune with Him. Every ignorance keeps us in the dark places, groping and stumbling at noonday. This is the average lifestyle of today's nominal Christian. When we stumble and hit the rock in such ignorance, we blame and grumble against God. Is it God's fault that men refused to take advantage of the light that is already come? He took the children of Israel through the wilderness one step at a time. The manna was supplied enough for the day so that they can go back to Him the next day. We need Him daily, every hour.

Your light is come, but you must choose to light it up yourself. That is the Gen-set. The power to choose is one undisputable privilege deposited in man from the first day of His creation. So, it is available to men of all races, status, and ages. Every man is free to choose, but the moment you make your choice, you become a slave to whatever action you have chosen. Our choice of actions forms our lifestyle and becomes what you call character. Even when you remain docile and do nothing about pursuing the right knowledge, it is still a choice. So, each time or day you settle for any choice of action carelessly, out of ignorance or from public opinion (including your NEPA-sources), you will stand responsible for the consequences. Every man will be judged according to his works (Rev. 22:12), and our lifestyle. So, you see how much we need this true, consistent burning light to guide our choice of actions daily. If our light has come; if the Gen-set is affordable, what then is responsible for our wrong actions?

DRAW FROM THE WELL OF FRESH KNOWLEDGE

Our wrong and/or inadequate knowledge is responsible for our wrong and unwholesome character, especially on spiritual matters. We saw many examples in the last chapter. We also have great men and women of God who displayed so much wisdom and faultless lifestyles both in the scriptures and in our contemporary world.

When Joshua took over the mantle of leadership of the children of Israel, the God of heaven warned thus: "This book of the law shall not depart out of your mouth, but you shall meditate therein day and night, that you may observe to do according to all that is written therein: for then you shall make your way prosperous and then you shall have good success" (Josh 1:8). This is the success secret revealed by God. What is the Father saying here? The Lord was telling Joshua not to depend solely on the ideas or on all that he has learnt under Moses.

Oh, they could be helpful, but more importantly you must continuously study this book of the law, you must meditate therein. Sit in my presence after studying the book and think, that is, allow my Spirit to interpret this book to you. "Joshua, there is a specific secret buried in that book designed to give you the divine illumination needed to guide your feet per day, per time, per victory. This secret can only be gotten in my presence. Your daily success draws from the well of fresh knowledge from the secret place." This is what I hear the Lord declare unto Joshua in my spirit man. The Lord declares the same today to the church and every believer that desires heaven ordained success.

If you have been sincerely having a good time in God's presence, you would have discovered that so many scriptural texts you thought you have known becomes new and fresh each day you are led by the Spirit of God to go back to them. What a mystery! This was the grace that kept the owners of the Gen-set alive and happy in the midst of the inadequacies of NEPA-LIGHT. They ensured consistent burning personally.

This kingdom walk is so designed that He must guide us each step of the way, else we find ourselves defeating stronger and mightier nations (giant-looking, opposing forces) only to fall prey to the smaller and weaker strongholds like 'Ai' (seemingly familiar spirits and temptations). See Joshua Chapters 7 and 8 to understand what went wrong.

When Moses led the wilderness church, he fell into this human problem of doing things as usual. He was faced with the same temptation to provide water for the people of God, as he had done before by striking the rock (Exd 17:6), not knowing that this time the Lord has changed the pattern. Speak to the rock was the new secret (Num 20:8), but he smote the rock twice (Num 20:11). The water came out, but Moses had missed it, and he paid dearly for it.

So many battles were fought and won by the children of Israel using various styles as directed by the same God. Sometimes, they fought from the mountain, sometimes from the valley, to demonstrate that the God of the mountain is the God of the valley. At one time, it was just the lifting up of the hands and the rod of Moses that brought the victory. At other times, the people of God sang praises, while the enemies destroyed themselves. When the whole army of Israel with all their armories trembled before the uncircumcised giant of the Philistines called Goliath, God discarded the trained warriors and armories of Israel, and used only David's catapult to bring down the giant. I can go on and on. He is the Lord! A song writer says, He moves in mysterious ways; His wonders to perform. This is why no mortal man can claim monopoly of God's knowledge. Don't be intimidated; get your Gen-set on and dispel every darkness of ignorance. It is our greatest undoing in this Christian faith – IGNORANCE!

THE GLORY OF THE LORD IS RISEN

The glory of the Lord is our divine seal in Christ Jesus (Col.1:27). The glory that was taken away by the devil when man was made a sinner rises up again with sweet radiance when man is made righteous at the new birth (Rom.3:23;5:19). But listen, this glory of the Lord radiates (shines) brighter and brighter, the closer and closer we get to the throne of glory. Rick Joyner confirmed this fact in the revelation compiled in his book – The Final Quest.

This glorious encounter marked Samuel out as a

different person from Eli and his sons whose religious leadership style lacked personal relationship with God. As he kept awake in God's presence to ensure a continuous burning of the light in the altar, the glory beamed unprecedentedly upon him on that fateful day (1 Sam 3:1-19). The inner altar-life was Samuel's secret, else he would have ended up another Eli, see verse 7. "Now Samuel did not yet know the Lord, and the word of the Lord was not yet revealed to him". In other words, he stood on the same platform or level of God's knowledge with Eli's sons till that day came. Compare that with 1 Sam 2:12, "The sons of Eli were base and worthless; they did not know or regard the Lord".

Samuel helped himself by personally ensuring that the light never got quenched. He employed the services of the spiritual gen-set. That is the mystery. Light begets light. As we personally create time consistently to lighten up our lives by dwelling in His presence, meditating and digesting divine precepts, His Glory automatically rises and shines upon and around us. This is the glory that illuminates our hearts with wisdom and revelations, giving us insight into mysteries and secrets in deeper and intimate knowledge of our God. This was Paul's ceaseless prayer for the church (Eph1:17). You can't beat any Christian operating at this level of knowledge.

Every saint that ever tapped into this secret that attracts God's glory remained outstanding. Listen to David at the beginning of his Psalms "Blessed (Happy, prosperous and enviable) is the man who walks and lives not in the counsel of the ungodly, nor stands (submissive) in the path where sinners walk, not sit down (to relax and rest) where the scornful gather. But his delight and desire are in the law of the Lord, and on His law (the precepts, instructions and teachings of God) he habitually meditates (studies and ponders) by day and by night. The man shall be like a tree firmly planted by the streams of water, ready to bring forth its fruit in its season; its leaf also shall not fade or wither; and **everything** he does shall prosper (and come to maturity)" (Psalm 1:1-3 Amp.). This is the mystery of the gen-set. It draws down and keeps God's glory when others are wallowing in obscurity. What are you waiting for? Leave the outer court and get into an intimate fellowship with Him.

Our prophetic text says ...darkness shall cover the earth, and gross darkness the people, BUT (for those that know their God), the Lord shall arise **upon you, and His glory shall be seen on you**. It does not happen by accident; it is your divine positioning that draws down His glory upon you (personalized) and marks you out. What a glorious estate! The Gen-set is the mysterious device that grants you access into Heaven's secret by keeping God's glory around you.

REVEALER OF MYSTERIES

The glory of God does not just come upon us only as a covering, but more than that it draws heaven down to fill our hearts. We live a tension-free life at this point because the issues that are supposed to put us under tension are being revealed and handled by heaven's wisdom which is supplied daily as we dine in His presence.

The greatest thing that man fears is the unknown. Every day of our lives, we are confronted with natural demands, spiritual and secular demands. When we are faced with such demands and we do not know how to go about it (that is, how to give a perfect solution to such demands), we are kept in the dark, and it will definitely keep us worried. Nobody enjoys a world of darkness. Every ignorance keeps us in a world of darkness.

We have often heard this quotation by the judiciary that 'ignorance of the law is no excuse'. That means you cannot project ignorance as an excuse for committing a crime. In other words, the law expects us to possess knowledge enough and commensurate with every stage of our lives else we pay dearly for it. This is why the man who does not want to die in ignorance must seek knowledge. That quotation was borrowed from the heavenly judiciary (Lev.4 and 5; Num 15:24-29). You now see that the greatest problem we have as Christians is our attitude to seeking the true knowledge of God. We do err often, because we do not know the scriptures or the power of God (Matt 22:29). This attitude bleeds the heart of God. We must leave the realm of ignorance fast. (Acts 17:30).

Why am I saying all this? In our God, every secret to all life's problems are discovered. Joseph knew Him in this capacity as the revealer of secrets, and He never disappointed him (Joseph). We all know the story of how Joseph became the Prime Minister in Egypt his land of captivity. It did not just happen by chance, nor by jumping up and down, commanding heavens to come down, nor by rehearsing the promises of God. He spent time IN HIS PRESENCE. He employed the services of his Gen-set in the midst of the gross darkness that covered Egypt then. It was a no NEPA-LIGHT situation. Read Genesis chapters 39-41. In chapter 41:16 (AMP), look at his answer to Pharaoh when he was called upon to give the interpretation to Pharaoh's dream. "Joseph answered Pharaoh, it is not in me: God (not I) will give Pharaoh a favourable answer of peace". Look at Pharaoh's remark after the interpretation in verse 38: "can we find this man's equal, a man in whom is the Spirit of God"? (Amp).

Faced with a similar NEPA-Blackout situation many years after in Babylon – his own land of captivity, Daniel stood before king Nebuchadnezzar and declared: "The mystery (secret) which the king has demanded neither the wise men, enchanters, magicians, nor astrologers can show the king. But there is a God in heaven who reveals secrets… and He who reveals secrets was making known to you what shall come to pass" (Dan 2:27-29,

Amp). After his interpretation, "King Nebuchadnezzar fell on his face and paid homage to Daniel …and said, of a truth, your God is the God of gods and the Lord of kings and a Revealer of secret mysteries… (Dan 2:46-47). Many other examples abound.

Brethren, God is very much interested in receiving this honour from the world around us. He deserves it all. This is why He is more willing to let down His glory shine upon us than we are ready to avail ourselves and acknowledge it. We don't need self-promotion and praise singing. When His glory is attracted to us as we consistently dispel every darkness around us through our spiritual Gen-set, mysterious secrets will be made known through wisdom and revelations. What follows next? See our prophetic text again – Isa 60:2, 3 "…and His glory shall be seen on you, and nations shall come to your light, and kings to the brightness of your rising." What a great privilege!

Stop running after spiritual power and authority. You cannot handle it until God has handled you in the place of HIS PRESENCE. It is the greatest debasement today seeing ministers of God and Christians going to occultists and witch doctors to ask for power. This practice has become so rampant in our time to our greatest shame. When we ought to be the center point of power by reason of our consistent burning witness through our personal, power generating sets, we are rather going to the world of darkness to seek for cheap powers.

Those of us who cannot stand the shame of resorting to the witch doctors like Saul, have settled for all forms of acrobatics, entertainment and massive, exaggerated advertisements just in order to attract and keep the people. Why? Simply because we have forsaken the place of His presence where we are equipped with the intimate knowledge of Him who alone remains the fountain that draws down every glory. We are running around with all the broken cisterns that holds no water. May God open the eyes of our understanding and recover us wholly.

It is not within the scope of this revelation to delve into the accompanying grace, power and authority to knowing God personally. Suffice it to say here however, that the benefits are sure and certain; they are better experienced than told. Just make a good choice now. Move away from the ordinary level, the peripheral level, the general knowledge level. Create time and seek to know Him personally. You will be dazed at His visitation.

8
THE POWER

Knowledge carries and wields great power or influence over its captives. It is wonderful when you become a captive of a coveted knowledge. Knowledge is power. Show me a man who is fighting a battle or pursuing a course of life with the last drop of his blood, and I will show you a man who has been personally persuaded and overwhelmed with the power of influence of the knowledge of that course.

When Paul came to this point of knowledge of God, he said, "I know whom I have believed, and I am persuaded that He is able to keep that which I have committed to Him against that day" (2 Tim 1:12). Nobody could stop him in the face of fierce oppositions. When he was about returning to Jerusalem, not even the opinion of other brethren with all their prophetic gifts could stop him. When all the brethren heard the prophecy of all that Paul was going to be confronted with at Jerusalem, they wept terribly, urging Paul not to go. But listen to Paul, "what mean you by weeping and breaking my heart like this? For I hold myself in readiness not only to be arrested and bound and imprisoned at Jerusalem, but also (even) to die for the name of the Lord Jesus. When the brethren heard this, they knew that this was beyond their level of understanding, they now stopped crying and said, the Lord's will be done" (Acts 21:13, 14. Amp).

In all ages, and even in our contemporary world, we have men and women whose acquaintance with the knowledge of the Lord made a nonsense of their personalities. They took their stand at various times, even against the majority opinion and at the risk of losing their lives propelled by the power of their personal knowledge of the Lord. They are unbeatable. Great Heroes of the faith!

Here, in this last chapter, I just want to challenge us with some historical facts from both the Bible and Christian books, excerpts of men and women who knew the Lord personally and how much their lives were affected by such knowledge. Compare them with what you are doing today as a child of God, especially when confronted with the little trials of our faith. I begin to wonder whether we are all going to share the same heaven with these great clouds of witnesses, or may be a different heaven will be created for some of us. How is this possible? We might be very familiar with some of the stories, but please employ the services of the Gen-set this time, meditate on these things and allow them minister to you personally.

SHEDRACH, MESHACH AND ABEDNEGO

"Then Nebuchadnezzar in his rage and fury commanded to bring Shadrach, Meshach, and Abednego... and said unto them, is it true? Do not you serve my gods, nor worship the golden image which I have set up? ...Now, if you worship not (my image) you shall be cast the same hour into the midst of a burning fiery furnace; and who is that God that shall deliver you out of my hands". Shedrach, Meshack and Abednego answered and said to the King, "O Nebuchadnezzar, we are not careful to answer you in this matter. If it be so, our God whom we serve is able to deliver us from the burning fiery furnace, and He will deliver us out of thine hand,O king. But if not, be it known unto to you, O king that we will not serve your gods, nor worship the golden image which you have set up" (Dan 3:12-18), That was the power of a personal, intimate knowledge of God. Their bold stand for their God taught Nebuchadnezzar the lesson of his life.

DANIEL

Daniel's personal knowledge of the God of Israel prompted him to take a personal but very risky stand in the land of captivity (Dan.1:8). Operating under the level of this knowledge, the Lion's den became no threat to him. He preferred being thrown into the den of Lions than stop having a good time IN GOD'S PRESENCE (Dan 6). This experience culminated into the secret that he revealed in chapter 11:32 which we examined in chapter one on this book. Even the Lion's den provided him a solitary place to enjoy personal fellowship with God.

STEPHEN

Unrestricted by men's appointment who thought he only qualified for the office of a deacon, Stephen died a fearless evangelist. He was overwhelmed by the knowledge his Lord and Master and ministered in that power. Stephen was cast out of the city and stoned to death in defense of the Lord he had believed (Acts 7). While he was being stoned to death, rather than curse those that stoned him like we would do today, he prayed for their forgiveness. This is the spirit-power of personal knowledge and conviction.

JUDE THE APOSTLE

Jude, the brother of James was commonly called Thaddeus; He was crucified at Eddessa A.D 72. His crime was that he defended the truth he believed. You can never die in defense of what you are not personally persuaded about. The gospel we are called to believe and to preach places a high demand on our lives. We cannot pay that price with the general, mental knowledge of God.

MATTHEW THE APOSTLE AND THE FORMER TAX COLLECTOR

As he laboured for the master in whom he believed at Parthia and Ethiopia, he was slammed with a halberd in the city of Nodobah at AD.60. What a price? The day he hosted our Lord Jesus Christ as a publican, he did not do it for showmanship. He truly turned his back at ungodly riches and turned his life to the Lord Christ and the kingdom life project. Matthew proved that the only course worth dying for is Christ and not riches.

JAMES THE LESS

He was beaten and stoned by the Jews, and finally has his brain dashed out with a fuller's club as he defended the gospel he so believed. The power of personal knowledge at work.

SIMON

Simon the Zelotes preached the Gospel in Mauritania, Africa and in Britain. He was crucified in A.D. 74.

LUKE

In defense of his knowledge of the Lord, he was hanged on an Olive tree by the idolatrous priest of Greece.

THOMAS

Thomas needed no other argument or plea, after inserting his fingers into the Lord's hands to feel the points where the Jews nailed and pierced Him. He became personally persuaded that he preached the Gospel in Parthia and India. He was killed by being thrust through with a spear.

BARTHOLOMEW

He translated the Gospel of Mathew into Indian language. He believed in that course so much that he died by being beaten and then crucified.

PHILIP

Philip laboured in defense of this great knowledge in Upper Asia and suffered martyrdom at Heliopolis in Phriga. He was scourged, thrown into prison and afterward crucified in AD. 54.

MARK

Mark was tied to a Horse and dragged around until his body was shredded in parts by the people of Alexandra as they celebrated at the great solemnity of Serapis, their idol.

JOHN THE BAPTIST

He declared God's word with such a resounding assurance and boldness, fearing no man but He whose shoe latchet he is unworthy to untie. Yes! John knew Him that much. He was beheaded by Herod (Mark 6:14-29).

ANDREW

Overwhelmed by the knowledge of the truth, he went on and preached in many Asiatic nations. He was crucified like his master, but on a transverse cross at Edessa.

JAMES

James the Great was beheaded by Herod in Jerusalem (Acts 12). His offence was that he declared the truth of the death and resurrection of Jesus of which he was an eyewitness. He stood his ground till death.

JOHN THE BELOVED

In defence of the truth: "That which was from the beginning, which we have heard, which we have seen with our eyes, which we have looked upon and our hands have handled of the word of life. (For the life was manifested. And we have seen it and bear witness and shew unto you that ETERNAL LIFE, which was with the father, and was manifested unto us); that which we have seen and heard, declare we unto you…" (1 Jn 1:1-3). "My testimony about my Lord, says John is a true testimony of how much I have come to know Him personally; as he declared this truth, he was cast into a cauldron of boiling oil under Domitian, he escaped by a miracle without injury. He was banished to the Isle of Patmos to be eaten up by reptiles and wild beasts, but they could not hurt him. In this Island, he wrote the book of Revelation in AD 96. In the Isle, he went through the revelation school of the Holy Spirit. What a power!

MATHIAS

Mathias was elected to fill the vacant place of Judas Iscariot. He was stoned at Jerusalem and then beheaded as he defended the gospel.

PETER

Peter stood by the power of the knowledge revealed to him not by flesh and blood, but by the God of heavens (Matt 16: 16, 17). He was crucified upside down; feeling unworthy to be crucified like the Lord, he asked to be crucified that way under Nero. You know what that means? When he was about to be crucified, he pleaded not to be crucified the same way his master was crucified. He rather demanded that he be crucified upside down on the cross, counting himself unworthy to die the same way His master died. It couldn't have been anything outside the inherent power of personal passion for a course.

PAUL

A greater part of the book of the Acts of the Apostles, and the epistles of Paul the apostle to the churches revealed a little of what he went through defending the Lord for whom he counted all things but loss for the excellency of His knowledge. Finally, Paul was led out of the city and beheaded under Nero.

In case you may be thinking that those great martyrs of the Christian faith that were mentioned earlier were only able to stand strong in defence of the truth, because they lived and dined with Christ, or because the fire of Christ's death and resurrection still burned fresh; how wrong you can be? How about those that made their marks before the coming of Christ? How about those that are making their marks today, smiling within and praying for their persecutors while they are being tortured to death for their defence of the Excellency of the knowledge of Christ? They all defended the faith with the last drop of their blood being inwardly persuaded by the strength of their personal, revelation knowledge of God. What a power!

The following excerpts were taking from the book 'TORTURED FOR CHRIST'; written by Richard Wurmbrand who spent over fourteen years in the communist jail. His crime and the offence of all these brethren was that they knew the Lord so intimately that the fire of communist torture could not deter them from the strong grip of such knowledge. May you be challenged today to go for your Gen-Set! That is the secret.

RICHARD AND HIS WIFE

When communism was introduced into Romania, thousands of priests, pastors and ministers did not know how to discern between the two (that is communism and Christianity). In other words, in the shallow understanding of those ministers, the communists appear to be preaching the same message with the Christians. This simply shows how much those ministers knew the Lord their God. What a disappointment? So, a congress of all Christian bodies was convened by the communists where about four thousand ministers attended. One after another, bishops, and pastors arose and declared that communism and Christianity are fundamentally the same and could co-exist.

Richard Reports: "My wife and I were present at this congress. She said to me, Richard, stand up and wash away this shame from the face of Christ! They are spitting in His face". I said to her, 'if I do so, you lose your husband, she replied, I don't wish to have a coward as a husband'. Then, I arose and spoke to this congress, praising not the murderers of Christians, but Jesus Christ… Afterward, I had to pay for this but it was worthwhile (p 6, 7). I had tortures in the prison that I prefer not to speak because they are too painful to account for, when I do, I cannot sleep at night. (P. 27).

TWO CHRISTIAN BROTHERS

Pushed by the power behind the knowledge of the Lord, two brothers (no title attached), pushed their way to the Prime Minister (Russian), Gheorghiu Dej, defying the wrath of communism that may follow. They witnessed to him about Christ, and for this daring witness, they were thrown into prison. Years after, when the Prime Minister became sick, those words the brethren pumped into him came powerfully and sharper than any two-edged sword (Heb. 4:12), piercing into his heart. He surrendered his life to Christ (p. 23, 24).

THE UNDER-GROUND CHURCH

Reporting on the activities of the Underground Church which existed like the Gen-set in our revelation in this book, it became necessary to keep the gospel light burning within the communist dark world, Wurmbrand said, "The Underground Church worked not only in the secret meetings and clandestine activities, but boldly in the open proclaiming the gospel on the communist streets and to communist leaders. There was a price, but we were and are still prepared to pay it". He went further to report that 'the communist persecutors knew that if a man believed in Christ, he would never be a mindless, willing subject. They knew they could never imprison a man's spirit and his faith in God. And so they fought very hard" (p.25).

UNSPEAKABLE TORTURES

A Pastor by name – Floresiu was tortured with red-hot iron pokers and with knives. He was beaten very badly. Then starving rats were driven into his cell through a large pipe. He could not sleep because he had to defend himself all the time. If he rested a moment, the rats would attack him.

He was forced to stand for two weeks, day and night. The communists wished to compel him to betray his brethren, but he resisted steadfastly. Eventually, they brought his fourteen year old son to the prison and began to whip the boy in front of his father, saying that they would continue to beat him until the pastor said what they wished him to say. The poor man was half mad.

He bore it as long as he could, then he cried to his son, 'Alexander, I must say what they want! I can't bear your being beating anymore'. The son answered, 'Father, don't do me the injustice of having a traitor as a parent. Withstand! If they kill me, I will die with the words, JESUS AND MY FATHERLAND'. Enraged by his stand, the communists fell upon the child and beat him to death, with the blood spattered over the walls of the cell, and in the presence of his father. He died praising God (P.29).

Brethren, these are no fictions, they are true life stories. Get the book and read; you will discover more heart-breaking experiences that men like us went through for what they believed. We praise God for the crumbling down of communism, but you know, some people paid dearly while it lasted. Let us take just one more challenge.

THE WEDDING GIFT

One of the Christian workers in the Underground Church was a young girl. The Communist Police discovered that she secretly spread gospels and taught children about Christ. They decided to arrest her. But to make the arrest as agonizing and painful as they could, they decided to delay her arrest a few weeks, until the day she was to be married. On her wedding day, the girl was dressed as a bride, the most wonderful joyous day in a girl's life! Suddenly, the door burst open and the secret police rushed in.

When the bride saw the secret police, she held out her arms toward them to be handcuffed. They roughly put the manacles on her wrists. She looked toward her beloved, then kissed the chains and said, "I thank my heavenly Bridegroom for this jewel He has presented to me on my marriage day. I thank Him that I am worthy to suffer for Him". She was dragged off, with weeping Christians and a weeping bridegroom left behind. They knew what happens to young Christian girls in the hands of communist guards. Her bridegroom faithfully waited for her. After five years she was released, a destroyed, broken woman, looking thirty years older. She said it was the least she could do for her Christ. (p. 33).

What a challenge! May I know Him enough till He becomes My Christ, not just our Saviour.

I did not add these excerpts to make up volume of this book, but to challenge us. Do you think you know God the Father enough to withstand such pressure of negative forces that contend daily to separate you from the love of God? I do not know how many times you have opened wide your mouth to talk anyhow to this faultless God or murmured against Him just because of a temporary setback.

Oh! You may have been having a good time since you got born again; that is wonderful! But just know that we will all face our trials here someday, in some form or another. So, don't get carried away with the good times, else you will be carried away by the wave of your own trial when it comes. Seek to get acquainted with Him now. Seek to know Him to that point when you can join the song writer to boldly say:

"My faith has found a resting place; not in device nor creed; I trust the ever living one; His wounds for me shall plead;

I need no other argument; I need no other plea; it is enough that Jesus died; and that He died for me".

It is this level of knowledge that generates the power in you to repel every darkness that hovers around you on a daily basis. Yes! That was the power that kept the early saints burning in the face of very fiery trials. We too can boldly hold our chests out in the face of temptations and trials of our time, than grumble and complain. We can declare like Paul the Apostle, "Who shall separate us from the love of Christ? Shall tribulation, or distress, or persecution, or famine, or nakedness, or peril, or sword? As it is written: "For Your sake we are killed all day long; We are accounted as sheep for the slaughter. Yet in all these things we are more than conquerors through Him who loved us. For I am persuaded that neither death nor life, nor angels nor principalities nor powers, nor things present nor things to come, nor height nor depth, nor any other created thing, shall be able to separate us from the love of God which is in Christ Jesus our Lord" (Rom. 8:35-39, NKJV).

It is a wonderful experience; it is very real! You cannot know it until you employ the Gen-set. Get into HIS PRESENCE. Get to know Him personally. This is the end-time secret to keeping you outstandingly alive, amidst dead men that seem to be on the high side in this generation.

This is the message the Lord desires to send across the entire body of Christ through that simple but pregnant dream. He reveals from the known to the unknown as that unbeatable teacher He has always been. What a God with whom we have to do!

"And this is life eternal; (this is the secret of kingdom life) THAT THEY MIGHT KNOW YOU, the only true God, and Jesus Christ whom you have sent", Jesus prays to the father; and this is my prayer for you as you have gone through this revelation.

Recommended Books For Studying When sitting In God's Presence

1) Knowing God Personally Vol.1 (The Intimate Dimension) By Godson Hez
2) Knowing God Personally Vol. 2 (Seeking Divine Perspective) By Godson Hez
3) Fresh Fire For Fresh Result By Godson Hez
4) We Need Revival, Not Survival By Godson Hez
5) Tortured For Christ By Richard Wurmbrand
6) Whose Image Are You By Lafamcall Ministries
7) Becoming Like Jesus By Gbinle Akanni
8) The Journey To The Wealthy Place By Ngozi Favour Anyaora
9) The Final Quest By Rick joyner
10) The Call By Rick Joyner
11) The Sword By Rick Joyner
12) The Path By Rick Joyner
13) I Dare To Call Him, Father By Bilquish Sheikh
14) And other Revival Books

www.ingramcontent.com/pod-product-compliance
Lightning Source LLC
Chambersburg PA
CBHW070108120526
44588CB00032B/1376